Natasha,

Thank you !!
Hope you will enjoy.
Isabel Canzoneri

THE AMERICAN DREAM AND
EVERYTHING IN BETWEEN

Diary of an Immigrant

Isabel Canzoneri

THE AMERICAN DREAM AND EVERYTHING IN BETWEEN

FIRST EDITTION

Editor: Annette A. Caton & Kerry Mcloughlin

Book Cover Design: Darryl Vickers

ISBN-13:978-1541080485
ISBN-10:1541080483

Isabel Canzoneri

TO MY MOTHER

THE AMERICAN DREAM AND EVERYTHING IN BETWEEN

Isabel Canzoneri

Table of Contents

ACKNOWLEDGEMENTS

There are many people I would like to acknowledge and thank.
First, I want to thank my family and my friends in Brazil, for all the support.

My siblings – Maria, Joao, Nilza, Cida, Sebastiao, Alceu.
My brothers-in-law, Dorival and Ronaldo and sisters-in-law, Lurdes and Marlene.
My nephews, Eduardo, Matheus, Leonardo, Natan and Felipe.
My nieces, Vanessa and Andressa.
Two special young ladies, Vanessa and Naiara.

I love you all.

A special thank you goes to both my brother, Alceu, who took financial care of my mother in my absence and his wife Marlene, who watched over my mother and acted as my personal assistant taking care of my business. I had peace of mind knowing they were there, a doorway for whatever needs my mom had.

A special thank you also, to my best friend and partner in life, my husband Stephen Canzoneri, whom I love dearly and my parents-in-law, Pat and Nick, who are a huge part of my life here in the U.S.. My parents-in-law are my best friends here.

I must also thank some other people and at the top of that list are Roderick Harron and Russel Radach—thank you so much for everything. Darryl Vickers, Sue Vicory, Blake Barber, Elaine Swann, Jeri Holst, Jocelyn Bruce, and my Agent, Pam Pahnke, you all have made a difference in my life here as well.

Thank you all very much!

RANDOM NOTES FROM THE AUTHOR

It is not easy to be an immigrant, regardless of which country you come from or immigrate to.

It's not easy for a country to support illegal immigrants—not only because it's very expensive, but because it's also dangerous.

Immigration has always been part of the history of every country. It's very important to understand all the things involved in the process.

All the things I went through before and after my immigration to the United States made me see things from another perspective…from different angles. It's scary and frustrating sometimes, yet it's very exciting.

Friendship is something very important in everyone's life. Friends help us go through whatever challenges we are facing, giving us support, encouragement and making us see the bright side of everything and above all, they accept us just the way we are. They always have a hand, a word, a shoulder or whatever you need—just for you. These of course are the traits of true friends and if you happen to have at least one, consider yourself lucky, as they are hard to find!

Never stop believing in you. You are here for a reason, whatever that may be. It's up to you to change the things you don't like in your life. Of course, there are things you will never be able to change, but it's still up to you to accept or embrace them to have a better life.

Be curious, search, play, love, give, inspire, accept, volunteer for a cause, reach out to someone in need, and learn to receive.

Live your life to the fullest. Life itself is a learning process. Go learn how to live yours and do not worry about other people's lives. They are on a different path and in a different stage than you are. Everyone has a different mission in life. Live your life. Improve your life. Eventually you may find yourself improving someone else's life—sometimes without even knowing it. Be kind always.

INTRODUCTION

IMMIGRATION

Talking about the American Dream and not talking about immigration would not make any sense for the thousands of people who dream about coming to this great country to make a better life for themselves and perhaps for their families.

Every year, many countries—and I will be talking about the United States especially—receive hundreds of illegal immigrants who cross the border facing all kinds of danger. Many do not make it and die on their way, drowning in the cold waters of the oceans or expiring in the harsh conditions of the desert, inside refrigeration trucks, in trunks of cars, or other ways I can't even imagine.

A lot of them are caught and sent to jail and later deported, losing their rights to come back legally as a tourist. Even if they are granted a Visa in their native country allowing them to travel again, they run the risk of not receiving permission to enter this country or not being able to stay due to their previous status. Many arrive at customs at the airport and have to go back to their country right way on the next available flight.

These people see opportunities to improve their lives, leaving countries that face terrible social problems and have little or nothing to offer them. However, living as an illegal in a new country can also cause that country to face social and economic problems as well.

Every time the subject of immigration is raised, it brings all kinds of questions, concerns, doubts. It's a constant concern for our government as it tries to deal with the situation. Whatever decisions are made on cases, they are constantly criticized by the people and by both parties in Congress.

Since that terrible episode in 2001 on 9/11, immigration has been a huge issue in this country. Policies for granting Visas have changed; security at airports has tightened for the safety of all travelers, airline crews, and all airport workers. Many travelers complain because of the long lines and invasive procedures they have to go through.

While all things seem to be easy in this country, in reality they are not. When people watch movies made in the US, they see all these beautiful cities and places, and they might wonder how it would be to live in this great country. It's only natural to want a better life.

Although I never had the American Dream that so many people talk about, I always wanted to visit this country and I had the opportunity to do that a few times before I became a resident in 2008. Later on, I became a citizen, an accomplishment of which I am very proud.

I never thought it would be easy to find a job when I moved to the United States. All my friends who came here and spent time pursuing their American Dream, or studying, could find only positions as au pairs, babysitters, housekeepers, pizza deliverers, servers, and other minor jobs.

I do not think these jobs are bad or make you less worthy than others who have higher level positions. On the contrary, people who have these jobs are very hard-working. Many manage to keep their dream alive. For them, hard work pays off and they are able live comfortably. Others, however, live from paycheck to paycheck on a very tight budget.

My story is different because I didn't come here chasing the dream, whatever that may mean, or to study or to work to start a new and better life. I never had that American dream in me. It was not my thing. Of course, everybody wants to have a better life. I'm no different than anybody else, but I was not looking for the American Dream.

I love traveling and as I said, I had come here a couple of times on vacation but I never thought about living here. And, that's not because I thought it would be difficult or because I would miss my family, friends, and country, which I do, or because I did not like it here. Who doesn't like here anyway? It was just because I never really thought about it.

I had an okay life in my country and despite everything bad that happens there—the terrible politicians that govern Brazil and don't take care of what they really need to be taking care of, such as education, healthcare and the environment among other issues—it is the place where I was born. It is where I grew up. It is the place where I went to school and made great friends. I was lucky to have a very decent job with a reasonable salary.

Despite everything, I still believe Brazil is a beautiful country with beautiful people. I'm not talking about the beauty the magazines and TV insists on throwing in people's face, leading people to do crazy things in the name of a beauty standard that companies and their marketing has set. I'm talking about people with a good heart. These are people whom, despite everything, always have smiles on their faces. People who have hope and work hard and make a good living. Sure there are bad people there too; they are everywhere. However, this writing has nothing to do with my country, its beautiful people and its issues. It's about my journey here. To be more specific, it's about my saga searching for a job.

As I said in the beginning, people spend lots of money—money they could use to open a small business in their country—to come here illegally to make a life for themselves and their families, thinking it will be easy. Perhaps, they even know it will be difficult but because their country has nothing to offer them, they hope their new life will be better.

It's not as easy as it seems and they should know that. Many of those people end up being homeless and hopeless. The American Dream might exist but is not for everybody. If you still believe it's easy, I invite you to read my story and see for yourself. Whether you have a proper education or not, it's certainly not going to be easy and even if you do have proper education, be ready to bring your level down. Every story is different and I don't want people thinking this is intended to be a model to follow. We are all on a different path, a different journey and this is my story and my point of view. This is not a guide on how to succeed or how to find a job here. It's about my own experience and I just felt compelled to share it with whoever wishes to read it.

While I tell you my story, I will also share a little about my life and my views on certain issues and the differences between American culture and our culture in Brazil.

CHAPTER ONE

TRAVELLING THE COUNTRY

I love traveling. I always did and I always find myself saving money to travel. I have done quite a few wonderful trips both in Brazil and abroad. It was in 2000 the first time I came here on vacation. I visited New York, Miami, and Orlando and I'm not going to lie—it was an amazing trip and I loved it!

It felt so unreal to be here. It felt like I had an out of body experience. I don't know how to explain this but when I was walking in Central Park, or the streets of New York, many times I felt myself coming back to my body. It's weird to think about it. I'm just trying to put in writing what I felt and it's difficult because I can't explain it. I found myself, or my mind, I should say, wondering around all the time. To me it felt like I was home, but obviously I was not. If you believe in past lives, maybe that could explain it. I just don't know. Maybe that's just how we feel when we realize a dream.

Now, please forgive me if I offend anybody as that is not my intention, but people in New York were not the friendliest people in the world. I know some people from that state, including my husband's family, and they are marvelous people. However, when I was visiting back then I met only grumpy people. They would not look in our eyes when my friend and

I asked for information—that is, if they would actually even answer any questions.

One time, we had just gotten out of a train station. We obviously were lost, with a map in our hands looking around to figure out which direction to go and we were trying to ask people information on how to get to a certain place and they wouldn't even stop to talk to us. A gentleman (from some place in Europe, I assumed by his accent), saw us trying without success to talk to the people who were rushing by, probably trying to get to work. He took pity on us and approached us asking if we needed help. We were super happy with the offer and after less than a minute, we were on our way to the first adventure of the day!

Anyway, it was not a pleasant experience as far as the people of New York City were concerned and I understand that sometimes we are stressed out about something and without knowing or wanting to, we are rude from time to time. Of course, there is no excuse to be rude to someone, but it happens to everybody, at least one day a year, well, more like more than one day. It just happens.

I also can't forget the fact that sometimes we women are just more likely to get hurt. Perhaps I was having that time of the month and of course, I also have to say, perhaps people didn't understand what we, well, what I was trying to say. You know…the language barrier. I can't say that I was a very good English speaker then, so I can't really blame them. Not that I think I'm an expert in English now—I'm far from that—but I'm sure my skills have improved a little after living here for more than nine years now. Yet, people sometimes still don't understand me or misunderstand and misinterpret me. Probably they don't understand me most of the time. I don't know anymore and truth to be told, I don't mind as much as I used to. I just try to be aware of everything when I speak. If people seem to be confused or mad, I try to make the statement in a different way and it seems to work.

Nonetheless, New York, for me at least, was just like São Paulo. The high buildings, all the cars on the streets, all the people, bumping at each other on the sidewalks while going to work, restaurants all crowded at lunch and dinner times and even the grey skies. I went in March and the weather was not too good but it was not bad either. It was actually, a pleasant weather.

Regardless of my bad experience with a few people who were not very welcoming, it really didn't change the way I felt about it. I really liked it. Perhaps it's because it reminded me home. São Paulo is in a way, to me, like New York City.

The architecture is beautiful! I loved Central Park. I was so impressed by the train station there! It's huge. If I was alone I would be totally lost… and let me tell you something, I was a little scared being at the train station, because I few years earlier, I had seen a movie about a creature that attacked people and in one scene it was in a train station! Man, that film gave me the creeps and scared the hell out of me… well any horror movies have that effect in me. I have seen a few of them and don't watch them anymore. I can't sleep!

Anyway, as a tourist, I visited most of the attractions, including the twin towers, which were standing beautifully at the southern tip of Manhattan for tourists to admire. I still remember exactly where I was and what I was doing when I heard about the tragedy that marked forever the lives of thousands of people in the world. 9/11 happened a year after I visited and I couldn't understand and will never understand such an evil act.

From there we went to Miami. When we got to Miami, I thought it was a beautiful city and found the people much friendlier than New Yorkers. I even made a couple of friends in the hotel lobby. While one of my friends decided to go out, my other friend and I decided to stay in the hotel and we went to the bar in the lobby. We had so much fun that night.

Anyway, there was a pianist who played for us all night, and the poor bartender couldn't go to sleep because we were there… I mean, not all night, but until my friend and I and the other woman we met at the lobby, Cassandra, decided it was time to go back to our rooms. This lovely woman from Miami was a caregiver and was staying at the hotel. The person she was caring for was wheelchair bound and was traveling so she would travel with him. She was an African American woman and she and I exchanged contact information. When I went back home I received a beautiful card from her in the mail. It was so sweet, and I called her to thank her and from that day forward, we were in contact, exchanging Christmas cards, birthday cards and letters. I loved to receive letters from her. In fact, before I moved here I wrote her a letter telling her that I was dating someone from here and she was happy for me. After I moved here, after seven years since we first met, we are still in contact by phone.

The first time I had the experience of filling up the tank on my own was in Miami! It was so exciting to do it myself. You know, in Brazil the attendants do that for you so I had no idea how to do it here. Can you imagine someone who doesn't speak the language and stopping at a gas station to find out there is nobody to help you?

Well, that's not really true, because every gas station has a mini market and if you need help, the cashier may be able to help you. Not sure if he is working alone if he can leave his post but, you may try.

It was fun to figure things out and learn how to do it myself. My two other friends had more experience traveling abroad than I did. I was the virgin traveler and of course, a picture needed to be taken. Tourists, aren't they funny?

Miami will always be in my heart. The beaches are beautiful! I especially liked Fort Lauderdale. I will never forget certain places there, like Fort Lauderdale itself, Miami Beach, Key West, Key Biscayne and Boca Raton.

On that same trip, we went to visit Orlando; sure, we had to go to Disneyland! Talking about Disneyland I need to share this with you.

My two friends and I woke up super early and drove from Miami to Orlando to go to Disneyland and we were so excited to be there. I was fascinated with how easy it was to drive here. Seriously, you can't get lost! In addition, the stop signs are a God's send. In Brazil, for you to cross an intersection is a nightmare, so good luck trying.

When we got to the Disneyland, we parked our rental car in this gigantic parking lot and off we went to discover the adventures of that huge park. We were like kids and well, we were not that young. I was about 30 years old.

At around 9 pm we were super happy and exhausted and decided to go back to our hotel in Miami. It would be a long trip, so we went back to the parking lot.

Guess what? We got to the parking lot, and we looked around us and saw a sea of cars and we had no idea where we had parked the car. Not a clue! We had not taken any note of the location.

Go ahead and laugh because this is true. Can you picture that? Three Brazilian girls completely lost in a huge parking lot looking for a white car. We didn't even know which brand it was or the license plate for that matter!

So we decided to split up and each of us went in a different direction looking all over the place, but how on earth would we find a white car without knowing the make or license plate number? It didn't go very well as you can imagine, especially, for the two of us who didn't have the key of the car. My hope was that my other friend who had the key would be luckier hitting the car alarm button so we could find the car.

We spent more than an hour walking around the parking lot and we only found it after most of the visitors had left and the three of us finally reunited and walked together hitting the button to find the damn car. We were so happy when we found it. We were exhausted but there we were, the three of us, laughing as hard as we could at our own stupidity!

One of my friends had driven the car from the hotel to Orlando and it was my turn to bring us back to the hotel and get us there safe and sound, hopefully. My friends slept all the way and I had a very hard time staying awake on the road. I turned on the radio to keep me company and stay awake, but it was really hard and I have to say that I feel like I fell sleep a couple of times while driving. I say that, because I woke up a couple of times, with eyes wide open at the sound of that noise that you hear when you start going off the road. I'm sure I just blinked but that is a very stupid thing to do. Driving when you feel like sleeping! Don't you ever do that guys, it's certainly not a smart thing to do. An accident can happen in a blink of an eye.

Don't ask me how I did it, but somehow I managed to get off the highway. Maybe I was sleeping! Looking at the rearview mirror it was completely dark and I rarely saw another car on the road. I stopped at a gas station to ask for information and my friends woke up but as soon as we were on the road again they went back to sleep.

Yep, all that happened and I don't know about my friends, but I never, ever park anywhere now without taking a picture of the location I'm parking in, whether it is a spot number or letter or animal sign. Never! Lesson learned.

We also went to the Keys while we were in Miami. My goodness, the road to the Keys was quite an adventure! Driving on a road with water on both sides of it was scary and super exciting at the same time. That, I will never forget for sure.

The nightlife in Miami was amazing and we loved it. Of course, I always go to bed early and it was great to find out that the nightlife here is very different from Brazil.

I loved it here… Everything closes earlier! When I tell my friends in Brazil that I have dinner at 3:00, 3:30, 4:00, or 5:00 pm, they think I'm crazy! I love this and I'm so in the right place! I'm not an owl, that's for sure! Thank God, my husband is like me.

In Brazil you go out for diner anytime from 7:00 to 10:00 pm. Dance clubs in Brazil are open from 8:00, 9:00, or 10:00 pm till 5:00 or 6:00 am! It's for party animals.

Anyway, there is one thing I thought was very weird in Miami. There were people walking on the street with huge white snakes on their necks! I would think, "*Are these people crazy to have a snake as a pet?*" I'm not very fond of snakes…at least I was not then. Nowadays I kind of like them… I mean, I don't like them, but I guess, because of my relationship with nature… you know, I love nature and they are part of it right? Plus, I know they will never attack you if you don't step on them or if they don't feel threatened by you and well, I guess, yes, I like them now and I think what influenced me was my nephew who became a Biologist. I'm so proud of him! Oh, and I even touched one the other day at a zoo I visited in Portland recently. It was a yellow and very thin one, with very soft skin. I was so surprised to feel how smooth it was… so cute too.

Some people are irresponsible and think it's cool to have a snake or exotic animal as a pet and then they find out they are hard to care for and simply release them—causing a huge problem for the environment. And don't get me started on having regular pets and simply abandoning them. This happens all the time, everywhere. Certain parents find it cute to give a child a bunny for Easter and then later find out it's a lot of work to care for them and abandon them. What do they think? Do they think that the poor animal will adapt and learn how to find food on its own if it never learned how to do that? Same with cats and dogs, especially cats, they buy the pets instead of adopting and they don't spay the animal and then they let the cat go out and it gets pregnant and has a litter and they just dispose of the poor babies! I can't talk about this. It's too upsetting.

I have my reservations about zoos. It was not always this way, I used to love them when I was younger, but as I grew up and developed my consciousness about animals, I came to a realization that I don't like them… I mean, not that I don't like them, I just don't like to see the animals confined in a small cage or space. It's not fair to the animals and I understand they have good intentions as they talk about conservation but in my humble opinion, it is more about the money they can make bringing people in to see the animals and that makes me sad.

However, I like those types of organization that welcome injured animals and take care of them because of their condition, because they can't take care of themselves anymore and therefore would not be able to survive on their own. I applaud what these organizations do to help them and to protect those animals. It's only fair for them, to be able to charge visitors a fee, as that is one way they can make some money, to help feed and care for these animals.

It makes me sad that we are here taking more and more space from them—the animals—chasing them out of their own territories and habitats, just as we did with the Indians! Please, don't get me started on that. All right, this has nothing to do with the reason I decided to write this book. These are only my personal takes on the subject, so let's move on.

From there we went to Cancun, Mexico. Talking about this, later in my story you will read some funny stuff about geography. I hope I will remember to include that. I hope you won't get mad at me because of it either. It's funny to think about Cancun and relate it to Mexico. Cancun seems to be a completely different country and yet, it is a part of Mexico. However, it's just because Cancun was better developed and the other

13

parts of Mexico, well, not so much. Cancun was developed with the wealthy in mind. Alternatively, should I say that Cancun was developed with tourists in mind...people who are willing to spend their money. Of course, I say that based on the fact that I visited mostly the downtown area, hotel circle and all the beautiful beaches and attractions Cancun has to offer and the beautiful parts of it. I have never been to any other parts of Mexico, so I cannot be a good reference. I want to visit other parts of Mexico though and one day I will. Viva Mexico! I love Mexican food and their people.

The second time I came to visit this country, I went to Louisiana and Colorado in 2004 and 2005, spending almost three months between those two states. I loved the food in Louisiana. By the way, the weather in Louisiana sucks big time. In New Orleans, I had a great time in the bars and restaurants. It was fun to see all those blues singers all over the place. In every corner and square, there was a group doing what they do best: playing and singing The Blues! The people were very nice too. I also loved their accents.

People in that state are very religious and a lot of them are very old fashioned. Although I think there is nothing wrong with that, it was a little too much for me, but I respect their views and beliefs. I'm talking about Baton Rouge here.

The one thing I didn't like there was the fact that it seemed to me that there is a very strong prejudice still going on within the population. At least in Baton Rouge, where I spent most of my time, I could see that as clearly as water. I don't know about now, but then there were neighborhoods only for black people, or should I say, African Americans and other neighborhoods for white people. I really didn't like that but I believe prejudice is something that still hasn't really ended in many places, including Brazil, and it goes back in history and I just hope it will end one day.

However, I also believe it's not only one side's fault. People put themselves in a position where the prejudice actually comes from them sometimes. For example, I heard a couple of times things like: *"what is this white trash doing here?"* Or *"I prefer to date a blond than a black girl,"* this coming from an African American man. It may be weird, but that's how I see things happening sometimes and this is something people, both sides,

14

need to work on. The prejudice is so strong in certain people that they reject their own kind. That's definitely wrong. Education starts at home. Parents are responsible for what they teach their kids and must be aware of their own words when talking to their kids, but more than that, of their attitudes towards other people and the world. You can't change people. You have to change yourself first to see a change in others. It takes time and it takes responsibility.

Moving on to Colorado, I saw snow for the first time and it made me cry. I have no idea why I cried, it just touched me and for no reason or a reason unknown to me. A mixed feeling invaded me. I don't really know what happened, but I think it was because I wanted my family, specially my mother to experience that. I wish they had been with me but I guess somehow, they will see those things through my eyes and my pictures.

I absolutely loved Colorado. It's a beautiful state and the people there were great too. I loved to stop by the cafes in the middle of nowhere on the roads covered with snow. The coffee tasted like my sister's... more like a tea. I loved it! People there were very fit. I would see people running, cycling, skiing, walking, hiking. They were very active people and into exercise. Colorado is the perfect place for those who enjoy being outdoors.

Anyway, the third time I came visit the US, I came to California.

To tell you the truth, I didn't think California was beautiful, at least it was not love at first sight. I looked at all the dry empty land. It really didn't appeal to me. I guess I was blind, because as soon as I started to see it for what it is, I realized how beautiful it really is, even with the desert part. In fact, I love the open areas. I mean, it's beautiful and there's no other place in the world that I would like to live.

San Diego is without a doubt one of the most beautiful cities I have ever visited. And the weather... ah, the weather, nothing can beat it and there is a saying there: "*You pay for the weather!*"

I didn't fall in love with Los Angeles, as I thought I would, perhaps because of the traffic and dirty parts of the city and the graffiti. Living in São Paulo for so long and having to spend hours to commute to work and school made me, I guess, create an aversion for any little traffic. And boy the traffic in Los Angeles is bad… maybe not as bad as New York City and São Paulo, but it's bad.

I liked California so much that the following year I came back again and spent a couple of days in Arizona and Nevada. I didn't like the heat in those places but other than that, there is nothing bad about them, although I really didn't see much there then so, I cannot tell. What do I know?

When I travel I like to see different places so you may be wondering why I came back to California. The fact is that, my husband (my boyfriend then), lived in Encinitas, which, by the way, is an adorable little town in North County San Diego, so that's the reason I came back the second time. There is always a reason for everything right? I totally believe that.

Steve asked me to marry him when he was visiting me in Brazil. We talked about how it would be living here, and I brought up the job issue and he assured me that I would find a job in a blink of an eye with the skills I had. I didn't know about that.

Every time people meet me, when they find out that I'm from Brazil and that Steve is American and doesn't speak Portuguese, they always ask me if I already spoke English when we met. And my answer for that is, yes.

Sometimes I wonder why people always think that in a country like Brazil or any country outside Europe and North America that the people are not capable of speaking other languages. Not that they are completely wrong as many people really don't, but at least in the main cities they do. Nowadays there are so many foreign companies in those countries that there is no way for people to work with them if they don't learn and speak English. Besides that, public schools teach English starting in fifth grade. It's basic, but it's better than nothing. Private schools start teaching kids in elementary school. I'm talking about when I was studying those grades, but I believe nowadays they learn English probably earlier.

Let me tell you a little bit about us so you get a better view of my story with my husband. When we met, I was working for a multi-national company in Brazil as an Executive Assistant and I had a very decent salary. Before that, I also worked as an Executive Assistant for another multi-national company for almost eight years and my salary then was even better. Unfortunately, the business didn't take off the way they thought it would and they shut down that first business. Well, it was not only that, but it doesn't matter now, but just so you know, it has to do with corruption.

While I was working as an Executive Assistant, I had a lot of contact with the Executives and Secretaries in the US, so I had to have good English skills, or at least be able to maintain a conversation, as I would speak with them almost every day over the phone, or when they visited for meetings and conferences.

I told Steve that it was not going to be as easy to find a job here as he thought it would be, but he was convinced that I could find a very good job, with a very good salary. He believed that not only because of all my experience working for multinational companies as an Executive Assistant and Events Coordinator, but also because I had a BA degree in Marketing and besides, I spoke three languages: Portuguese, English and Spanish. He thinks I speak three languages. I do speak two and I can communicate in Spanish, but for him I speak three. He tells everybody I speak Spanish very well. It's so cute. Fine with me, I will take that but I'm not that good in Spanish. I understand everything people say when they are talking as long as they don't speak too fast. I can read and understand everything, but my speaking skills are limited by vocabulary.

I told him that my friends had the same skills and all but, even though they had great experience in their fields they would have to start from scratch here and he would say that I was being too negative, so I gave up trying to convince him otherwise.

We were in this long distance relationship and he visited me a couple of times and used to call me every day or almost every day for a year.

In 2007, I quit my job and a month later, I was on my way to California to spend some time with him and see if things would work out for us. We didn't know how we would feel about each other. Dating over the phone and visiting a couple of times a year was not an ideal situation as you can imagine. You only know someone if you live with that person and sometimes, not even then.

THE AMERICAN DREAM AND EVERYTHING IN BETWEEN

I thought it was cool to have a boyfriend in another country. So here I was, visiting him again after he visited me a couple of times. He took me to some nice places and I fell in love with San Diego County! We went everywhere and he showed me all around. Some of the places he showed me included Balboa Park, La Jolla, Old Town, Del Mar, Encinitas, Oceanside, Dana Point, Murrieta, Los Angeles, Beverly Hills, Santa Monica, Santa Barbara, Big Bear, Julian and Lancaster. That's a lot of places.

He also showed me all the posts on Craigslist looking for Executive Assistants, reading the job descriptions and asking me if I had those skills, which I always said yes to as I had experience in everything the companies were looking for: PowerPoint presentations, Excel spreadsheets, Word documents, Adobe, Outlook, Agenda, Minutes, Flight/Hotel Reservations (National and International), event coordination, luncheon planning, letter drafting, proofreading…you name it…I knew everything!

Plus, as per my husband, my boyfriend then, I spoke three languages. Therefore, I definitely had what it takes to find an awesome job with a great salary. Why wouldn't I find a great job? Well…

CHAPTER TWO

What Happens in Vegas...

I bet you completed the above statement. It's such a cliché, right? One day while I was visiting, Steve took me to Vegas. I had never been to a casino before and we stayed at the Bellagio and visited other hotels too because they all are very interesting places—an attraction themselves. The lights at night have always fascinated me. Try to see a city during the day and then watch it at night. It's so beautiful. It can be the ugliest place during the day but at night, looking from afar, they seem to be so beautiful.

It was so hot and dry in Vegas. It was summer time!

While we were there, Steve took me to a very nice restaurant and asked me to marry him, right there, right then, at that time! I never thought I would do something like that but there he was, so handsome, his beautiful blue eyes shining like a bright star. I could see his love for me in them, with a beautiful smile on his face, holding a beautiful wedding ring. He asked again, as it took me awhile to realize he was serious, and with him looking at me from across the restaurant table waiting for my answer, I said *YES*! And just like that, I was Mrs. Canzoneri the following morning!

That was crazy, I know and I never thought I would do something like that, and yet, I had just done it. Besides jumping out of a plane at a high altitude hoping the parachute would not fail, that was indeed, the craziest thing I had ever done. Perhaps those two actions are comparable with each other! I had a feeling of excitement but at the same time, I was a little scared. In fact, it felt the same way, as I was about to jump out of that plane some 15 years ago.

It was a weird feeling. There was no one from our family with us in that little chapel. It felt unreal and after we left the chapel, I kept looking at my finger and the ring trying to make sense of what we had just done. We were married!

We came back from Vegas and started the immigration process immediately with a lawyer. I could not leave the country while they were processing my papers and that scared me a lot because I had my entire family in Brazil and I was afraid that if something happened to them, especially to my mother, I would not be able to go see them. In addition, I was afraid that the "immigration people" would come after me. I know this is funny, but a long time ago, I watched a soap opera in Brazil and there was a girl, who came here illegally and paid someone to marry her. Of course, later she went to jail because her husband's ex-girlfriend denounced her to the immigration authorities, and she was found and deported. Surely I couldn't compare our situation, as she was an illegal immigrant, which I wasn't, but that didn't prevent my mind from spinning on the subject. Perhaps I should write a screenplay…

My new life started and I pretty much depended on my husband for everything…and I mean everything! That was somewhat scary because I had taken care of myself my whole life. I started working when I was only thirteen years old. My family was not rich and I never took anything for granted. My father passed away when I was a little over one year old and my mother had to take care of all her kids. We were eight kids! The oldest was 17 at the time of his death. I was the youngest.

My Godmother wanted to adopt my brother and I but my mother wouldn't give up on us. When they asked her, she said, "*I go hungry but I don't give up on my kids.*" Thank God she didn't give up on me or who knows how messy I would be today, feeling rejected and all. She worked so hard on the farm with my oldest siblings. It was a hard life for them. Only three of my siblings didn't work in the farm, the youngest ones…two brothers and I.

Anyway, when we came back from Vegas, Steve took me to the DMV to get a driver's license. Believe it or not, and I'm ashamed of sharing this one…I didn't pass the practical driving test. I was so upset! How come? I used to consider myself a great driver. All my friends thought so too, at least they used to tell me that, although I suspect they were a little scared of the way I drive. But tell me, is there a person who drives, who really trusts other drivers? I certainly do not and keep my foot on an imaginary break when I'm in the passenger seat. I only relax after I see the other person's skills behind the steering wheel.

Well, it turns out I was driving too slowly, in fact, below the speed limit! Here I was, trying to be careful, diving below the speed limit, trying to look like a very responsible driver and I failed the damn test.

Today I laugh about it but then, I was so mad at the rude woman who gave me the test. She could have said that I was driving too slowly, but no, she probably wanted to see me fail. Not everyone, but sadly woman tend to do that to other woman sometimes. It's like they don't want another woman to succeed, or perhaps they are just afraid the other will have more success than they will. Insecurity, or whatever you call it, is so wrong.

I came back home all upset and rescheduled the second test for two weeks later. On the day of the new test, I was waiting in line for my turn and I could see the woman that I took the first test with. I wanted to go there and beat her up! Seriously, well, not really. I would never do that but I was still upset with her. And I was thinking to myself, *"if this lady is my 'judge' or whatever they call them, again, I don't know if I will be able to control myself. I will certainly say something to her after I had my signed approved test in my hands, that was, of course, if I passed…"* I was terrified of her being my "judge" again, as everything could go wrong, because I had all these negative feelings about her. If I did fail again, I would tell her to be more friendly and nicer to people. I would tell her to give a smile to the people she works with. Just because she is in a position that allows her to give pass - no pass to someone, doesn't mean that she needs to put on a mean face. *"I bet a lot of first time drivers would be so scared that they would be nervous and not pass the test because of her bad mood."* My mind was working against me. I could have tried to talk to her after that first test… well I did… she didn't bother to answer so I got the message and shut up.

21

I was relieved that I didn't have to drive with her again. She was not a pleasant person to be around, that's for sure. Well, this is one side of the story…she has her side too and I have to respect that. We can't ever judge anyone. Anyway, this time it was a nice older African American man who said *"Good morning,"* with a beautiful smile on his face. That made a huge difference! It didn't cost him a dime and it was priceless to me.

He was so cute. We chatted all the way. I took the test as if I was not having one. I told him all about the woman that applied the test the last time and he told me that many people complain about her and that nobody in the department liked her. He said that she was like that to everybody. I felt sad for her and even said a little prayer for her. She must have a reason to be that way. We can never judge anybody, as we don't know what is going on in their lives. I felt bad about my poor judgment and I'm not ashamed of admitting it and revealing it. We are allowed to make mistakes, and we should learn from them. We are just human beings. A takeaway from this: Be kind always.

I received a provisory driver's license and I was good to go and get lost in California. Driving here was a huge difference. There is no traffic comparing to the traffic in São Paulo. That was of course, a great thing… and the stop signs to cross a street are amazing as I said earlier. In Brazil it takes forever for you to cross a street depending on the day and time. Nobody stops for you unless on roundabouts. To enter a freeway there is ridiculous and a line of cars forms behind you. It's not an easy task if you want to enter the freeway—you have to push your way through which is not easy if you are not an aggressive driver. In Brazil you have to be aggressive, otherwise you will be yelled at all the time by other stressed drivers. There is no way to not to be stressed out in the traffic in São Paulo!

Oh, and talking about traffic, here in the U. S. if you disrespect the rules and cross street in certain areas where you were not supposed to, you may get a ticket for jaywalking, if caught doing so by an authority. Well, maybe I'm dramatizing things a bit but it's a so much easier for pedestrians to cross streets in the U.S.. It should be like this everywhere. Pedestrians must cross streets only when and where it is safe and appropriated to do so. Drivers have to yell the right for the pedestrian wherever there is a cross walk and sometimes they do that even if there is no crosswalk and it's a tranquil street. It's another world. I call it education.

From time to time, I hear my husband and other people complain about traffic and I can't imagine what they would think about that in Brazil. That is traffic. Well, I know what my husband thinks about it. He hates it and in fact, he never drives in São Paulo. I wrote about the traffic there in one of my blog posts. Yes, I write blogs too. Most of my blog posts are about places to visit in Brazil. I visit hotels and write about them posting on social media and I have fun doing it.

So here I was, all happy, driving all over the place and proud of myself for not getting lost so often without a GPS. I have to admit that I have no sense of direction and people tell me, *go East, go North, go five miles and then turn Northeast*. That doesn't mean anything to me, unless I have a GPS in the car telling me where North, South, East or West are. Even then, sometimes I make a mistake. I'm telling you, I'm a lost soul.

While driving around the neighborhood where I was living, I always saw lots of stuff in front of the houses, with a sign it saying it was free. I saw all kinds of things. Desks, beds, coffee table, sofa, chairs, tables, clothes, microwave, stove, washer and dryer, refrigerator, bookcases and all kinds of other things. I could not believe it.

Oh, and many people use their garages to store things here. They are not for cars!

CHAPTER THREE

Culture: The Differences

People are often surprised that most Brazilians live with their parents until they get married and if they don't ever get married, well, they still live with their parents, most of the time, like let's say eighty percent of the time, maybe even more.

Honestly, I don't see much difference between us living with our families versus the American way, which is living with roommates. The reason that happens is the same as here, to save money and share expenses, right?

Personally, I don't see myself living with a roommate. With a family member, yes, but with a stranger, hum, I have my reservations. However, that's just me, I'm not judging anyone. It's just how I feel and think.

In my view, many people here buy houses that they can't really afford then they find roommates to help them pay their mortgage. I know many people who live in a beautiful home and have three or four roommates that pay rent in their houses so that they can afford to pay their mortgage and eventually pay off their home. I guess, I could say this is a smart move of their part, but that's definitely not for me. I want my own space and if I can't afford it, I will never buy it and I will be totally fine with that.

Maybe I would think differently if I had kids, as I would probably want my kids to have a home and everything I didn't have when I was a kid. Although, I don't think I would give them everything just because I didn't have things. There is nothing wrong if you have to work for what you want. It's actually healthy for you.

Of course, there are those people who buy their homes and then, unfortunately, things change and they find themselves in the middle of a financial hurricane and have to do something about it. Having a roommate is one of the ways they are able to continue to pay for the mortgage and to live the lifestyle they want or can afford.

I'm sure if I lived here alone, I would probably have to go that route—not buying a home, but renting a room at someone's house so I could afford to live here, but to tell you the truth, I would not like that, and without a doubt, that would be my only option. And I know this is the only option for many, many people living here, American or foreigner.

I think I would be unhappy living that way, though. You see, I understand that this is only a matter of opinion and this is mine and sure, my mind could change too due to circumstances. I'm just not used to the idea of a roommate, that's all. Perhaps I would even like it.

Some people say I'm too blunt. See, I say many things without thinking through them, but I say things anyway and assume the consequences. Many people don't like me because I'm too honest so sometimes, I prefer not to say anything. I'm sure people misunderstand and misinterpret me too. Interpretation is different for everyone and when it comes to a second language, that's even more prone to happen.

Regarding the differences between Brazil and the US, another thing that grabs my attention is that everybody lives with his or her boyfriend or girlfriend. The reason, I'm guessing is the same: to share expenses and save money…and probably to have sex, as a bonus! Correct me if I'm wrong.

Let's face it; it's really not for the sake of love. I'm not saying they don't love each other, but I'm sure the reason is much more financial than love itself. So I guess, people think, "*if I will have to live with someone, why not with my boyfriend or girlfriend?*" I don't think they are wrong thinking this way and, they get to know each other better and decide sooner than later if it's a good idea to get married with that person. So let's say that they have a trial period.

I can't even say that money is their reason, I mean, how could I? I'm just thinking and writing my thoughts as I go, and as I have said, I say things without thinking. I'm writing this book as if I'm talking to you. That's a crazy thought, but there you have it. My talking before thinking is working in writing. I guess I could delete it but then, it would not be real or fun for you, the reader.

Back to the people living together, there is nothing wrong with that. Besides, marriages have the same concept. It's a financial institution, as many people say. Do you want to argue with me about that? Take a divorce for instance. It becomes a couple's worse nightmare. Again, I'm not saying people don't get married for love. Of course they do, but sooner or later, it becomes clear that the couple benefit from each other's money and God forbid one day they decide to end the marriage. Please, don't' get mad, I'm not generalizing. Some couples are great and don't let the money interfere in their relationship, especially when it comes to their kids. But I know plenty of couples who live in a complete nightmare due to fighting over money.

That's not very common in Brazil, I mean, for girlfriend and boyfriend to live together. The marriage-divorce-money subject is the same everywhere. But I guess it's becoming more common nowadays in Brazil too, for couples to live together. Things change over the years and people are more open about their relationships. And there is absolutely nothing wrong with sharing the bills with someone you love.

Here are a few interesting facts for you about Brazil as far as the subject of boyfriends-girlfriends living together or apart.

In most cases, if a guy lives alone, he probably won't want to have his girlfriend living with him. You may ask me why and I may say that's probably because he would probably cheat on his girlfriend, bringing another girl, a one night stand perhaps, to his place…

Although most of the more experienced guys who live alone and don't want anything more serious with someone, would never take a girl, a one night stand type, to his sacred place. Why would he do that? That's why motels exist in Brazil. Oh, you probably don't know anything about motels in Brazil if you are not from there. I wrote a huge blog about that too.

Motels in Brazil are not the same as the motels here. They are mainly for couples to go and have sex! There, I said it. See, we don't need a boyfriend or girlfriend roommate for that. Although you guys save a lot of money for that matter.

If I lived alone in Brazil I would not want my boyfriend to get used to coming to my place just to have sex. Believe me, that's exactly what he would want. Why not? As I said, that kind of situation save the guys money and, truth be told, that's exactly why they live alone. That is, to bring all the girls they want if they are not interest in commitment. It will certainly save them a lot of money. There, I said it again!

So, there are a couple of interesting scenarios here: Scenario one: guys who live alone and have a girlfriend still want their privacy and freedom, perhaps to bring a one night stand to their place, from time to time.

Scenario two: guys who live alone and have a girlfriend and bring only their girlfriend to his place and if they want to fool around with someone else, they will take that someone else to a motel.

Scenario 3: guys who live alone and don't want any commitment with a relationship and who want to be able to bring whomever they want to their place as I said before.

Scenario 4: guys who live alone but don't want to bring anyone to their place and instead uses the motels.

So, with all that in black and white now, I have to say that I'm not sure why people are so surprised when they find out a 40 year old or older person happens to still live with their parents. I've met countless people who are older than that here who live with a roommate and to me, there is no difference. Just that in our case in Brazil, we live with our family and here, people live with roommate.

So let's agree that there is no fundamental difference, except for between the cultures themselves. And I'm glad I cleared that out so we can move on. Wait, not before I talk about something that I always get a little confused and even sad about. I don't understand certain things and this one is huge for me.

Because we live with our parents in Brazil, we take care of them when they get old. We don't send them to a nursing home. Some people, a very few people do, but it's mainly because either their parents got dementia or are very ill and they can't be home alone anymore and the son or daughter has to work and doesn't have time or doesn't have anyone who can do that job for them. Most of the time they try first to find a relative to help them and if they can't afford to pay a professional to come to their house every day and stay with the parent, then they do that. It's still a sad situation, but it happens sometimes.

But here there are a lot of nursing homes and parents move to one of them, when they feel they can't take care of themselves anymore. They say they don't want to be a burden to their kids. Did they forget all the sacrifice they did for their kids? I don't think they forgot but I bet the kids did. To me, this is a very sad situation. Good thing they have money because nursing homes here are extremely expensive. I have no idea what they do if they can't afford that.

I understand it's the culture here but it's hard for me to take in all that. I could never send my mom to a nursing home. Yes, I moved here and left her there, but when I left, she continued living with my sister and my brother, and my younger brother and his wife were taking care of her and besides, she was not ill or dependent of us. She was retired and she was still active and healthy.

I talked a lot with my brother before I made my decision as I wanted to make absolutely sure that she would have all the help and support she needed. It was only after long emails and conversations with my brother that I decided to make the move.

I also kept paying for her health insurance after I moved here. I left money in my bank account there, for this specific reason, and when I got married here, and sold my car there, I used the payments I received monthly to continue to pay for her health insurance.

28

When my money there was almost gone, I didn't know what I would do if I couldn't find a permanent job here, so that I could send money to pay for that. My brother took over that responsibility, and for that, I can't thank him enough. I didn't want her to be without health insurance, but she certainly couldn't afford to pay for it herself with her retirement plan.

After he did that, I kept offering to help to pay for any expenses he had with her, which he always refused saying that he had a very stable financial situation, and that I had done enough and that now, it was his time to help. We shared the same feeling about her being taken care of, and that's what made it easier for me to be here with peace of mind.

When my older sister retired, it was even better so my mom would have someone home with her all the time and that too, was comforting to me. Besides that, my other brother and his wife and son, lived one street away, and he used to stop by every weekend. He used to do that even when I lived there.

My entire family is very close so we were always at each other's places. My sister, who lives in a nearby city, used to visit at least once a month and used to call my mom almost every day.

That's what my mom always told me every time I called her, when I was living here and even when I was still living there, when I called her during the day from work, she always told me that my sister had called her too.

My sister from Parana, the state I was born in, used to visit us every year or at least every other year and still does and that was great. My mom loved her visits. She also used to call my mom very often.

CHAPTER FOUR

Marriage

Now, let's talk about my sex life. Nope, I'm just kidding. That's not going to happen. What happens in bed, stays in bed…oh, wait, that's not right… that's Vegas.

Anyway, I've heard that married couples go through an adaptation phase. When you get married, you have to adjust to the other person's life. It's the only way to survive in a marriage. I've been married for nine years now and boy, this thing called marriage is a roller-coaster!

Let's start with groceries. Supermarket time was an issue in the beginning. That was something that my husband and I had some disagreements about and some adjustments to get through. He was used to eating processed food. In Brazil, we are not into that, at least not at that time. You know, Brazil and other countries eventually copy everything from here.

In the beginning, it was a nightmare to go to stores with him. It was something I never looked forward to because I knew we would fight, well, not really fight, but we would argue and I would get upset. But I know it was part of the adjustment of marriage…and that adjustment is especially difficult in a bicultural marriage.

In Brazil, we eat homemade rice and beans every day with lunch and dinner. Not those packages of ready to eat rice they sell in supermarkets, nor those canned beans, which are ready to eat as well. We buy and make our rice and beans from scratch. The first time I cooked beans here, the water never got thick like our Brazilian beans. Seriously, it drove me nuts, and it took a while until I finally found one brand that worked.

The meat! Oh Lord, what is wrong with meat in this country? No matter how many spices I add to it, there is no taste! In Brazil, our meat is so tasty... no spices needed and it's delicious. But never mind, because I don't eat meat anymore. It's part of my new thing—a vegetarian trial—as I love animals and I just can't eat meat anymore.

In my mind, I think it would be okay if everybody eats a piece of meat every now and then, but every day? It's ridiculous when I tell people I'm vegetarian and they ask: *"How do you get your protein?"* Or they say: *"You are not going to have enough vitamins... You are going to be anemic."* And those are only a couple of the things people say. Ai, ai, ai... don't get me started on that.

Anyway, a month after our wedding we went on a honeymoon trip to Hawaii. Honeymoon... How people come up with these terms? Well, it was lovely. It was the first time I travelled on a cruise. I was scared but if I'd known it was so cool, I'd have done it before! I loved Hawaii!

When we came back, my husband went back to work, where he would spend two and a half days at work, come back home, and then stay four days and a half days at home. He worked Sunday to Tuesday, from 6am to 10pm Sunday and Monday and from 6 am to 2 pm on Tuesday so the rest of the days I would be alone--which I absolutely loved. It was the first time that I had real privacy and could feel as if I lived alone. Not that I didn't want to live as a couple, but seriously, I never had that chance before and it seemed to be a dream come true.

Some people can't stand to be alone. They do everything to break the silence. They turn on the radio or TV just to hear some noise, but I love it! I love the silence!

Anyway, as I've stated, in Brazil kids leave the house only when they get married or when they buy a house or rent when they have reached financial independence. Even then, they do these things later, probably in the late twenties and even older.

If they leave earlier, it's because of a job or such, where commuting is not worthwhile. And of course, I couldn't afford to buy a house, which was a serious consideration on my part before I decided to spend some time here. I had been saving money and I had even paid to reserve a unit in one apartment in Brazil. However, I was only doing that to be closer to my work, not really to cut the ties with my family and become independent.

Anyway, while I was waiting for the immigration papers to be processed, I would spend my days getting to know the area I was living in, going to supermarkets just to check the food and other products they have. Here they have so many different types of food that it's still hard for me to choose things. There are all kinds of bread--way more than in my country. There is more variety here, except for when it comes to fruit. Brazil has more variety. And my goodness was it expensive! I couldn't believe the price of fruit here!

Anyway, what I wanted to say is that, when I went to the supermarket with my husband, I didn't really have a chance to do that because he was always in a hurry. I've never been with someone so restless. It was another adjustment for me for sure. And I thought I was impatient!

There were all kinds of different prices and I never understood them before we were married, because I really didn't have much time to check things out. I remember when I was visiting my husband, when we were still dating, we went to the supermarket a couple of times and I kept looking at those price tags some of them yellow or red tags and I asked Steve, "Why the difference?" He told me it was when the products were on sale. When he got to the cashier to pay for the groceries, I remember they asked him if he had a card with him and when he said no, they always offered their card, to which he always replied, "No, thank you."

Then, the first time we were married, wait a minute, we only got married once, so let me start this over. This language thing…see, that's why people misunderstand me or have a look on their face that makes me want to laugh when I see their confusion.

When we first went to the supermarket together after we were married, and we got to the cashier and she asked if we had their card and Steve said *"No,"* and again denied to get one, I asked if we had to pay for the card. She said *"No,"* so I said *"Yes, I want one."* He got a little impatient because I had to fill out the form, but I did it anyway and got the card… she finished processing the bill after adding the card number. When she removed the receipt and read the receipt, she looked at Steve and said, *"She just saved you $26 with the card."*

I sensed a tone of triumph in her voice, perhaps, even a little sarcastic. She did it with a little smile on her face and she totally made her point to him. Today he doesn't go to the supermarket without the card. I'm a keeper guys, what can I say?

Come on, I'm not going to pass up any opportunity to save. My money doesn't grow on trees. So yes, I'm the type of person who uses the coupons they send us in the mail, why not? If you don't use them, you are losing money.

So, that day I learned that the little red and yellow tags I used to see on the shelves were promotions that only the people who had their cards could take advantage of to get the discounted prices. If you have a card you will pay the promotion price, if you don't, obviously you pay full price.

I consider myself an observer. I observe everything. I love to watch people doing their thing…*ai for Christ's sake, not that thing!* Sometimes I wonder if I'm being watched as well. I like to see people talking to each other, although nowadays nobody talks anymore. They and their cell phones are best friends…inseparable and even when they are with someone they keep constantly looking at their phones. That's so rude but I don't think people realize it. It's just the world that we are living in now. Another thing I found quite interesting is that the parents nowadays let the kids rule their lives. Don't get me wrong, I don't think it's only here. I'm talking in general now.

Many times at the supermarket, I see parents letting their kids get whatever they want. I mean, yes, I was very deprived when I was a kid and my mom couldn't afford to give me everything I would like to have, but that didn't make me a resentful person and I'm certainly not spoiled brat.

Yes, some kids make a scene at the supermarket if they don't get what they want and this is all on their parents. I wonder if the parents give them whatever they want just to escape from the embarrassment or because they want their kids to have what they probably didn't.

When I was a kid, if my siblings or I misbehaved anywhere, my mom would simply say things like *"If you don't stop, you will see when we get home."* Oh, and we would really see and feel it.

I'm so thankful for the way I was raised and today I see kids threaten their parents if they touch them. People will consider it spanking if you touch the kid. Of course I'm not talking about abuse like some kids go through, I'm not crazy! That is a real crime and should be punished by law.

Kids should not be spanked but a little slap on the hand or butt when they are little doesn't hurt and used to do wonders when I was a kid. Please, don't tell me that this is absurd and that I'm out of my mind and should go to jail just for saying that. I'm sure a lot of people my age and older will agree with my position. That's how we learned how to behave well and respect others, especially the elderly.

Nowadays it's rare to see kids getting up when an elderly person boards a bus or a train. Where is that kind of education? The education that my generation and beyond had. *Hey, wait, that make it sound like I'm old. Well, who cares about how old I am?*

The other day, I went to the supermarket and while I was shopping a lady passed by me pushing her cart with her son screaming like anything. She was trying to talk to him and he wouldn't listen to her and kept screaming to at the top of his lungs. Of course everyone was staring at the poor woman who was trying not to create a scene or be further embarrassed. An older couple who saw the show passed by me and the man was saying to his wife, *"That's child abuse!"*

The woman hadn't even touched the kid! She also didn't yell at him…so how was that child abuse? A guy that was coming my direction and heard the man saying that, looked at me and said, *"That's not child abuse, that's parental abuse…and everybody else around abuse for all of us having to see and hear that screaming!"* I had to laugh at his statement and I didn't say anything but I have to agree with him.

When I turned a corner a couple of aisles later, where the kid had started screaming, the same lady with the kid passed by me again and the kid was happy with something in his hands. She probably went around the aisles and came back to the section where he had started screaming to give him what he wanted so he would stop yelling as if he was being beaten.

It seems like kids know how to get exactly want they want because they are the ones who control their parents. Oh well, that's none of my business anyway.

Anyway, sometimes I go to Los Angeles by train to meet my husband and we come back together in the diamond lane. The diamond lane, by the way, is a lane on the freeways that you can drive in, only if there are two or more persons in the car. It's great. I think he uses me for that! Just kidding. I usually go when he has an event to attend or we go to see a show at Fairfax or if I have some business to do in LA.

Anyway, I went to LA by train about a month ago to meet my husband and I had to get off at Union Station to take another train to Burbank. I love to go to LA by train. The ocean views are amazing and besides, it's traffic free. Anyway, when I entered the train, there were many seats available…but not really. Everybody had their purses, briefcases, backpacks in the seat next to them. That's not very thoughtful.

I found a free seat and as I'm an observer, I watched the people entering the train and looking around for a seat. Not finding any seats available, they would move onto another car. Well, this lady came in and walked all the way from one door to the next, and nobody stood up for her to take a seat. She had a cane and walked with difficulty.

I did what was the right thing to do, just as my mom taught me when I was a kid. The woman sat down and thanked me. There were plenty of empty seats but all of them were filled with personal belongings, so I stood up by the door and another girl came and like me, stood up by the door.

The train left the station and got to the next one. Other passengers entered and the same thing happened. People would just move to another car. I couldn't resist and did something I never thought I could do.

I moved closer to the people, drew a deep breath in and said:
"Excuse me. May I have your attention please? I'm sorry to interrupt but I have to say this." Everybody looked at me. *"Do you know why we are standing here? Actually, I'm talking on my own behalf, I really don't know why she,"* and I pointed to the other girl, *"is standing but I imagine it's the same reason I am."*

"See, I don't think you even realized that many people walked through this car trying to find a seat and moved on because nobody would even look up. You all have your personal belongings in the seat next to you and it's so wrong. People should not need to ask you to move your stuff for them to be able to take a seat. This is public transportation. It's the end of the day and we are all tired, so please, have some consideration for others. You must be tired too. Your belongings should be under your seat or on your lap."

At this point a couple of people started grabbing their belonging and putting in their lap. Two people moved their stuff and offered me a seat, to which I said in response, *"Thank you, but I'm getting off at the next station. Thanks for listening and sorry for interrupting."*

The woman whom I gave my seat to started clapping. At this point I felt my face burning and I was a little shaky but I was feeling great as I knew, at least those people who were there, would probably learn their lesson and hopefully won't do that again.

The train got to Burbank and I got off feeling a bunch of eyes on me. I thought of my mom because one time we were on a bus and the bus was super full so we were standing and nobody gave her a seat. At some point, the bus came to a sudden stop, and my mom fell onto a man's lap. He pushed her back up and said, *"Get off me!"*

I got so angry! I grabbed my umbrella, and hit him in his shoulder and yelled at him to respect my mother, that she was more than 70 years old, and should be treated with respect and that she didn't do that on purpose. After the incident, a gentleman gave his seat to my mom, which I thanked him very much for.

I was so angry …I think I could have beaten him up! I kept looking at the first man in a way that was almost an invitation to fight. I stared at him all the way, until we got off the bus…and I'm just a little thing. That was not very classy, I know, but I don't have cold blood. I'm Latina! My dear etiquette friend would have covered her eyes and ears.

I never forgot that incident and my mom would remember that from time to time. She would say all the time that I had hot blood, that I was little but I was tough. Just the memory of her saying that brings a smile to my face and makes my eyes shine.

Sometimes I see people in a restaurant and they seem to be together but each are texting someone else. And they sometimes even show the other person what's going on in their virtual world. Whether it is work or not, they could at least have the decency of putting the phone away to have a real in person interaction. Have people forgotten how to be present?

The other day, I was with my husband at a sushi place that we go to every week and a couple arrived with their three kids, ages around 4, 8 and 9 perhaps. They sat, ordered and every one of them except the little girl, got their phone out and started doing their own thing. The boy was playing a game, the other one put his headphones on, the father and mother, who knows what they were doing on their phones. The entire time we were there, they didn't talk once and the poor little girl, kept trying to get the mother and the younger brother's attention by hugging them, by reaching her little hands and arms to their arms, shoulders, hair... eventually they would look at her and smile or pet her head but nothing more than that. It was sad to watch. Is this technology good or bad for relationships? I think in the sense that it's separating people it's bad, but again, that's just my opinion.

I love elderly people. There is something about them that I love, and maybe it's their wisdom that I admire so much. I love to watch them. Sometimes I feel sad because sometimes they seem so lonely. Of course, maybe they are not, and it's just my imagination. Perhaps I'm reflecting and projecting my own feeling on how I would feel at that age doing things like that, alone. As I said before, I love being alone, just that sometimes people seem to be so lonely.

There we go again, I'm getting off track. I think I'm too emotional sometimes. My family calls me "melted butter" because I cry very easily...even when I'm watching cartoons. I remember many times when we were all watching TV and a sad scene came up. Everyone stopped watching TV to stare at me and before I knew it I was crying and they were bursting into laugh. I love my family!

As I could not work until I received my work permit, I spent many days alone, navigating the net, checking out ads for jobs opportunities. When I was not doing that, I was going up the street and watching the ocean from a cliff a block away from my house. Many times, I saw the dolphins surfing the water. That's what it looked like they were doing, playing and having fun. I love to see animals in their habitat. They seem so happy and for sure, very alive!

Other than that, and walking around the neighborhood, there was not much more for me to do while I waited for the immigration process. That process was not so smooth...

CHAPTER FIVE

The Visa's Drama

When we got married, we had to submit documents to change my status from single, to married and resident.

The first package we sent got lost by the carrier so the lawyer called to let us know and he said we had two options: wait a little longer or send another package. My husband decided to send another package because he was afraid I would have a problem with immigration. I asked him to wait but the lawyer agreed with my husband and thought it was the best thing to do. So be it.

While I had to wait for the law office to send another package for us to sign, I entered into my secretary mode and called the carrier to try to find out where the package was. They had no idea what had happened to the package. They simply couldn't locate it. It sounded like it was stuck in some facility but they didn't know where and why, and they said they would give us our money back. So I gathered the receipt and sent them an email requesting the reimbursement as both the carrier and the lawyer had instructed. Later, we received our money back from the carrier for the lost package.

Then I called the Immigration office and they confirmed that they hadn't received anything. So, again, instructed by the law office, my husband canceled the checks we had sent with the first package.

A couple of days later we received the new package from the lawyer, signed it and added another check to the package. We drove to the office the following day to return the papers. Steve preferred to do that instead of mailing it.

A couple of weeks later we received a letter from the immigration office acknowledging that they had received the package and were processing the application. They informed us in the letter that we would receive another letter after processing the documents and that we'd be given instructions for further steps we would need to follow.

After a couple of weeks we received another letter from the immigration office telling us that our check didn't go through and if they didn't receive the payment they would cancel everything that had been done. Any approval they had given, if any up to that point, would be considered void. Of course that check was from the first package we sent.

I called the lawyers to inform them about the new letter we'd received. On the following day, the lawyer called my husband to tell him that we needed to send another check or they would cancel the other package as well, and the process would be delayed even more and I would have to take the risk of having the visa denied.

Without talking to anybody, I called the immigration office and explained to them what happened, that we'd submitted a package and it got lost by the carrier so we sent another package and that the check that was cancelled was from the lost package. The attendant said there was nothing she could do and if they didn't receive the check in a week the process would be cancelled and we would still need to pay the fees. It was $1,200.00. I didn't tell Steve because if it was up to me, I would let them cancel everything and if I had to go back to my country that would be no problem and we would just have to wait for the time of processing another application. Steve didn't want that to happen because during that time period I would not be able to come here and the period for processing the paperwork would take from six to eighteen months. They could even prevent me from ever coming again or deny my fiancé a visa because of the lost package and payment issue.

A week later, we received a letter, like the first one, from the immigration office saying that they received our application and soon they would send us a communication for me to go for the fingerprints. I checked the numbers of the application in both letters and they were different. That was from the second package so I called our lawyer and asked him to stop one of the processes. He called back saying that there was nothing he could do. He said he talked to them and they said we needed to pay.

He said that we could wait if we wanted to see what would happen or pay for the other application and try to get reimbursed. To me, this was ridiculous and nonsense. A scam, that's how it sounded to me. How come The United States of America didn't have control of names they put into their system? How come they received two packages from the same applicant's name and address and everything else and they didn't have a system that shows when they add a name to the system that it's already there? Didn't it show that there were two people with the exact same information? Instead of checking it further they just went ahead and processed both and charged for both? This was unacceptable to me especially as I had called them, and so did the lawyer, explaining the situation and giving them the application numbers in the letters! It was so wrong.

I had held the US in the highest regard, and thought of them as the best in everything. Now I had proof government systems were the same everywhere. They were getting the information through the phone calls and lawyer's letters communicating about what had happened. So they had all the facts and were still not willing to take care of the problem the way they should. Unbelievable!

My husband asked the lawyer's opinion on the matter and he said that this had never happened to him before and that if we wanted, we could wait to see how the process would develop but there was no guarantee. We decided to wait and we kept receiving letter every week threatening cancelation to a point that Steve couldn't take anymore and decided to send the check because he feared my deportation. I was so upset because he sent the check again. It didn't make sense to me. All they had to do, with me and the lawyer calling them, and sending them letters, was to cancel the first application. But no, they wanted the money!

With all the stress we were going through, with two packages being processed at the same time, with one processing smoothly and in accordance with their rules, and the other one, constantly bumping along on its way, and with the immigration office threatening to cancel everything they had done until that point, I was very disappointed.

Three months after I got married, my work permit arrived and the funny thing is that even though they had received and cashed the second and third checks, they never contacted us again with instructions on how to do the fingerprinting process for the second application. Now, don't tell me they didn't know they were processing two applications for the same person. Bullshit! Excuse my French.

I never heard back from the immigration office about the reimbursement and I still think about it and get upset because I truly believe they should have reimbursed us. They charged us twice, regardless of all the letters and phone calls informing them about the problem!

They cashed both checks and never bothered to reply to my letters or resolve the problem when I called…and I called many times. I don't think I will ever forget this and every time I think of immigration, it will be the first thing that will come to my mind. I think it traumatized me! I even wrote them another letter in 2013 about the reimbursement. Of course I never heard from them in response to that letter either. And I sent them copies of both letters! I still call that a scam.

Anyway, enough of this Visa subject, it still upsets me too much. The "forgive and forget" thing is not working for me with this issue. I know I should forget it, because it's not going to serve me in any way. Perhaps now that I'm writing about it, I'll be able to really move on. I feel I'm finally letting go. Only time will tell…

CHAPTER SIX

Job Search - The Saga

Now that I had my work permit, it was time to take action. I used to spend entire days sending my resume to all the ads I would see on Craigslist and also applying on companies' websites. That process would sometimes take me more than two hours…just to fill out all the forms and do the online tests for one application! Before I knew it, three months were gone and nothing.

Then I started applying for jobs such as waitress and babysitter but they asked for experience! I was so upset at this point. I guess I could have said that I had that experience in Brazil but I never did because I feared they would check my information. How stupid and foolish I was.

I knew in my heart that it was not going to be easy to find a good job here because my friends who came here to study English had the same experience that I had. Some of them even had a higher education level than I did and all they could get was minor work.

Not that I'm diminishing the value of these professionals; on the contrary, I think they work very hard and are honest people trying to make a better life for themselves. And I'm saying this again because I want people to understand that it's really not easy to be an immigrant.

The thing is, in my mind at that time, I had put all the effort and money into having a college degree in my country. I'd had a very decent job with a very good salary, so I didn't want to go back and start everything over. Believe me, I'd started at the lower level and worked my way up a little. I'd been happy with what I was doing then. It's just that it bothered me that I had to do it all over again. That thought had not crossed my mind. Going back to school for another degree was not a plan for me either.

It felt like I was having this battle inside of me. Every day I would think about the four years I spent waking up at 5:00 in the morning, commuting to work, working all day, and then from there, going straight to college. Then, taking a couple of buses back home, arriving after midnight, having dinner and going to bed… just to wake up again the next morning the same time and start everything over again.

So I refused to go back to school. In my mind, I didn't want to accept the fact that I would have to go back to school here if I wanted to do better and succeed, whatever success means. I was so upset and disappointed that I didn't see that this would be essential.

That was not the only thing I was battling. I couldn't believe the price we had to pay to go to a college here. It's not that it's not expensive if you go to a paid college in Brazil, but there, you don't need to pay thousands of dollars upfront or have a loan on your back before you even have a job to be able to pay for it. There, you pay monthly and, if you fall behind in payments, you can still go to college and finish your education. They give you the option to negotiate the debt. Of course, I'm sure that if I had asked my husband to finance me he would have, but how could I?

I had provided for myself and paid for all my own needs since I was thirteen years old, so I didn't want to accept the fact that if I wanted to go back to school, I would have to ask him for money and that, again, was not an option for me. I just thought it was not fair, so I couldn't ask that. I could have transferred money from Brazil, but I didn't want to take that money away in case my mom needed it.

In December 2007, I applied to work as an usher for Cirque du Soleil. I love Cirque du Soleil! I had seen one of their shows, "Alegria," in Brazil, but I had no idea what an usher was or did. I went to Google to see what the heck that was about. Oh, okay, customer services (I had experience with that too), seat people and give them information when they asked, etc... that I could do. I applied for it.

I went for the interview at an Employment Agency when they called me, and they gave me all the information about the job. They said they would call me if the Cirque's personnel decided to call me for another interview. So far, so good. I understood everything they had to say and, most importantly, they'd understood me.

The next step, if I was lucky, was that I was going to have an interview with Canadians. That's scary! I would speak with Canadians...and their accent! I was afraid I was not going to understand them and consequently that they would not understand me either because of my own accent!

Okay, so the agency called me a couple of days later to inform me that Cirque's personnel would like to talk to me and we scheduled the interview. On the day of the interview, I thought I was prepared, as I had read everything about Cirque and all its shows, the cities and countries they were present in and the places that they would go on tour. Of course I could not memorize everything, but I felt confident that I knew quite a bit about the company and the position. I had done my research well.

I got to the office and there were a few people there already, as my interview was scheduled for mid-morning. As I got there about fifteen minutes early, I could see that there were a couple of people leaving, including the person that was in the room when I arrived and the one that went in right after I arrived and I was thinking, "Wow, that's a quick interview." In my head I started wondering things like what if they didn't like me, what if I didn't know what to answer, or, worse, what if my answers were not what they wanted to hear?

I was next and the fact that I knew in advance that there would be three people in the room for the interview, asking me questions and watching me and then judging me, didn't really take way my fear. It made me feel even worse.

I opened the door and the room itself was intimidating. It was an empty room with three people seated on stools and another regular chair in front of them. *That doesn't look good to me*, was my first thought. I put a genuine smile on my face and said, *"Hi, good morning."* They responded and I approached the chair and extended my hand to each one of them and with a firm handshake, trying to look all confident outside but in fact being all shaky inside, I said, *"I'm Isabel Canzoneri, nice to meet you."*.

And they start talking…*OMG what were they saying? What were their names? I'd already forgotten their names…come on, Isabel, they just said their names…well, I never heard those names before…I will never understand their accent! I'm crazy, here I am in a triple job interview and my mind can't stop wandering around. Come on, Isabel, focus. Listen to them…they are speaking English after all! Oh, okay, that's not bad, I can understand them well. Actually, I can understand everything they say. Good. Great! YAY! But I did forget their names though.* I could not stop thinking. *What is wrong with me?*

They asked me how I was doing, how was the weather, probably trying to break the ice and make me feel comfortable, and it worked. I felt more relaxed, although being on a chair at a slightly lower level didn't make me feel really that comfortable. They asked what I knew about Cirque and I told them about the two shows I had seen. Then they asked about my work experience in Brazil and then they asked me about Brazil. It was a nice fifteen-minute interview and when it ended, I shook their hands again and genuinely thanked them for their time and the opportunity and said it was nice to meet them. Then I was out of the room and they were asking for the next candidate to enter the room.

Great, two interviews already for the same position for the same company and not one positive answer yet! And this was only for a position as an usher. I could only imagine how long and hard the process would be for an Executive Assistant position.

On the following day, I received another call from the agent and she said they wanted to move forward with me and a couple of weeks later, I went for a group interview somewhere in San Diego on a Saturday morning.

Of course I got there before everybody else so I waited in the car. I didn't want to be the first one to arrive, especially, before the interviewers. Two more people arrived. They didn't look like they were looking for a job. Well, they might be the workers for the Agency's office. I waited five more minutes…a guy arrived…he seemed as lost as I was and he was definitely dressed for an interview. He looked around and decided to stay in the car too.

Okay, now it's time to go in. Fifteen minutes for the interview, time to go in. I read a lot about how to dress for an interview, what time to arrive, etc., not that I didn't know about those things but I wanted to make sure I was going to be fine…so it was time to go in.

Of course I was the first to arrive and the girl was still setting up the room for the interview/meeting. She came to greet me and asked me to sign in and sit down.

I sat down but it was driving me nuts seeing her working, so I offered help and she accepted. She passed me the papers and asked me to set them upside down on the desks. I finished and looked at the table, and there were a bunch of other piles of paper, and she was moving around and I asked if she needed anything else and she said, *"I'm going to hire you as my assistant instead."*

I said, *"Great, when do I start?"* We laughed and she gave me more papers.

The guy that arrived after me entered the room and she asked him to sign in too. He did and came to the door, also asking if we needed help. Help was accepted and I gave him the papers this time, as I was closer to him. I was feeling as if I was the office manager! Darn, that was I used to do when I worked as Event Coordinator. Why couldn't I find something like that? I miss that craziness of event coordination!

We finished and I found a seat. Little by little the room was filling up. Oh, I saw that guy at the office when I went for the first interview and that girl too. Maybe I should sit next to them. He probably read my thoughts and he sat next to me and said, *"Hey, you were at the office when I went for my interview."*

Ah, someone nice! His name was Art. He had a Cirque du Soleil jacket on and had like three or four Cirque ID on his neck. We start talking and I was glad I was not the only one with the accent there…he was of Mexican descendant. Another immigrant and that reminds me of my immigration process and unfair double payment. I'm telling you, I'll never forget this. All the room was quiet except for Art and I, who were yelping like we knew each other for years.

The woman from the agency came in, welcomed us all and thanked us for coming and there went my mind again. *What is she talking about? Of course we would come. We need a job, desperately! This was our chance! A foot in the door!*

Now, that she talked a little more about the position, she invited the three interviewers from Cirque du Soleil, introduced them by their names and they took the lead from that point.

They talked about our role, how important it was because we would be the first and last impression of the Cirque family. They told us that we would deal with all kinds of special people. Some very nice and some, well not so much, just like everywhere else, but, like every customer service person, we would always have to agree with them at all times but at the same time, be firm to them if they pushed us and any problem we had with them, the supervisor should be called in. Most important, always treat them with respect.

I looked around and everybody was paying attention as if there would be a quiz at the end of the presentation. I was taking notes as well.

After they told us what our rules were, the salary and the problems we would face, they asked for those who didn't want to move forward to leave. Two people left the room. I don't know if it was because of the salary or they would not put up with people yelling at them and be cool with it or if, like me, they couldn't understand very well what they were saying because of their accent! Whatever their reasons were, it was none of my business anyway.

Then they asked us one by one to introduce ourselves and let them know why we would like to work as Cirquadors. That's what they called the ushers or anybody working for Cirque du Soleil. That's nice, I would be a Cirquador. Isn't it cute?

My time to talk arrived and I was still thinking about what I was going to say when they called my name... Oh, yes, sure. I stood up and... *"Hi, my name is Isabel Canzoneri and I'm from Brazil. I used to work as Executive Assistant and Event Coordinator. I moved here last year to get married and now I'm looking for a job."*

48

They congratulated me on my wedding and I continued as they kept looking at me. *"The reason I would like to work for Cirque du Soleil is because I absolutely love their shows and, above all, I respect Cirque for not using animals in the shows to make money with them."* They said thank you and asked me which shows I had seen. I was so glad I didn't lie and, proud of my knowledge about Cirque shows, I said, *"Ah, I saw Alegria in Brazil and O in Vegas."*

One of them said, *"Awesome, thank you Isabel,"* and called the next person. *What? Well, could they say something else… like, great you are in but they said nothing…* so we heard everybody else's introduction and the interview was over. They thanked us all for coming and told us they would make a decision and if we were selected the Agency would call us back to schedule an appointment on the site job for training.

And there my mind started working again. *Are they going to hire me or are they going to say thank you but you don't have what it takes to be part of the team? Why am I thinking all this? Relax, tell the truth and you know what, if they don't want you, they will be the ones that will lose.* My mind seems to never stop thinking!

One week later I received a call from the Agency. I was in. Cirque would be in San Diego (Del Mar Fairgrounds) in January, or was it February? Whatever, that doesn't matter. What matters was that I was going to work in the US for the first time since I moved in six months earlier! And I would be an usher for Cirque du Soleil. That was great and I was happy.

They scheduled another time with the Cirque people so they could train us before the show. That training was scheduled for a week before the show started. So here we go again, this time at the site where the shows would take place. Another Saturday, all day this time and there I went again. This time was different. It was more relaxed as we were already hired. Aww, what a great feeling! And this would be a paid training! YAY…making money even before work starts. Score! Well, not really. For meeting in different sites and far from my house, gas is not free, so I considered that as a reimbursement for my gas.

And there was Art! He recognized me and came to talk to me. Great, now I have a little friend and I will stick with him, as he has a lot of experience working as Cirquador. The good thing is that he seems to like me too. Now, he met another guy, JC, who had worked with him in another Cirque show. Great, another friend! He introduced me to JC and the three of us were kind of inseparable. JC was an African American and older than me. Very cool gentleman. He immediately started singing Garota de Ipanema for me (the girl from Ipanema). Cool, he knows something about Brazil. Later on you will find out in this book that JC and I were connected again through another organization, a non-profit I had the privilege to be a part of.

They showed us the behind the scenes and we saw the artists practicing, their costumes, and technicians. It was very dark underneath the bleachers, where artists have to move around to change costumes or have to run to the other side of the stage.

One week has gone with me sending my resume, applying for jobs on the internet and the first day of the show Corteo arrived at Del Mar Fairgrounds. We, the ushers, were all dressed in black, just like technicians. There is a reason for that. We will be working in the dark, moving around and being dressed in black will not distract the audience from the show. We will watch the mast posts where the technicians will go up and down and we have to be behind them to protect the cables that they drop so people will not trip on them and fall in case they go to the restroom. Or, if they are seated behind the post, we have to be behind them and watch so if people stand, we have to make sure they won't bump into them or the ropes. Bottom line: we are there for safety reasons.

We have a quick meeting before we open the doors for the patrons to come in and check out the merchandise and food tent. Doors are open one hour prior to the start of the show. Not the doors for the people to go inside the tent where the shows are performed though, only the door that grants them access to the concession tent, where they can buy food and merchandise. The door for the performance opens 30 minutes prior to when the show starts and we are ready inside to open them, and start seating the guests.

Five minutes before the doors open, I'm terrified. *Will I be able to take these people to the right section and seat in the dark? Oh Lord, help me.* The small doors have two ushers and the big doors usually have four or more sometimes.

The Supervisor yells, *"Open the doors!"* and we run to our positions. One goes to open the door and the other or others stay in position to greet the guests and take them to their seats. In the beginning, it's easy because the lights are on. Although, for people that come from the outside, it's pretty dark until they get their eyes adjusted, so we need to watch out for them, so they don't trip on the steps and fall.

Of course most people arrive almost at the beginning of the show because they know they have reserved seats and we are screwed because of that. *Oops, pardon my French*. We have to rush and there are a bunch of people waiting on lines inside the tent now. Ushers are running around, almost bumping into each other, checking their tickets to see seats and sections and to take guests to their seats. Some people come to the wrong door and obviously wrong section and then, my friend, we have to send them to other door, through the inside or outside, depending on the time. They get mad at us, of course, because it's our fault that they came to the wrong door.

If we don't have many people in our doors waiting to be seated, we may rush — well, when it's possible to rush — with them to the right section and hand them to the usher in that section to help them out.

There comes trouble. I check some tickets and give a quick look to the row were they were supposed to be and oh, no! There is no available seat. I take their tickets and ask them to wait there and push myself to the seats, trying not to disturb the others as much as possible and I ask to see the tickets of the people seating on their seats. They have same seats, same row! *What now? Calm down Isabel, think. Check the dates*. Great, wrong day. I asked them to come with me and explain they had tickets for another day. They get frustrated and disappointed and I tell them I would call my supervisor to see if there are available seats for that day.

Meanwhile, I ask them to wait by the door, while I take the other guests to their seats. The guests that were waiting anxiously are now super happy and thank me for having their seats back.

Someone with a radio had called the supervisor for me and they come and, of course, look for me as I was the one who had requested them. I explain the situation and they take it from there. There are people waiting to be seated, and there I go again. The group with the tickets with the wrong date thanks me and is escorted to the box office by my supervisor.

With all those things going on, we needed to watch out for kids or people to stay away from the path where the clowns that are distracting the audience before the show starts are performing their acts.

Lights start to dim, clowns go back to underneath the bleachers, where there should be an usher to open gates for them and prevent people from mistakenly or willingly entering the area. There are so many cues to pay attention to.

Once the show starts, we can't seat people anymore, except at the very end of an act, which you will know by cues.

Before or during the shows, with all the other things going on and that you have to pay attention to, you have to go after cell phones or cameras. People are not supposed to take pictures or film the performances. I don't know how many times we have to go in the rows, disturbing everybody to get to the cameras or cell phones. Due to the excitement, people usually don't pay attention to the announcement in the beginning of the shows and we have to disturb those who do.

Fifteen minutes after the show starts, some ushers go for a break. When they come back, it's almost time for intermission and some ushers go to stay in position in front of the stage, or behind the posts so the technician can come back down safely or without stepping on someone's head! While guarding the stage, we give information for many guests who come to ask us all kinds of questions. Like, how many trucks are necessary to move the tents and all the equipment, how many days does it take to set up and break down, how many artists are there, are we followers or locals? Yes, we can follow Cirque from city to city and work with them. It's on our expense though. I would love to be a follower but, as I was married, I never did! Plus, I would probably have to make arrangements and live with a roommate, which that idea never appealed to me.

Show restarts and the ushers that still didn't go for the break go now. Many people rush to the tent for the second part of the show, but if when they arrive the show already started, they need to wait until we let them go back to their seats again. The good thing about this is that now we don't need to take them, as they already know where they were seated. Of course there is always someone that is not sure so we help them out; and there are the ones who get mad at us for holding them by the door to wait for the right moment to let them go back to their seats. Don't you just love customer services?

End of show we have to gently, push out, the last group of people that remain in the tent. Everybody out and we close all the doors from the inside and start cleaning! Yes, we have to grab all the trash left behind: cans, popcorn, hotdogs, candies, sodas. We have to empty all liquid in buckets and take it to the bathrooms. We separate recycling and trash. You wouldn't believe how much popcorn and other food are thrown away.

We take all the personal belongings that people leave behind to the lost and found boxes that are kept by the security personnel in their tent or office.

After we sweep the tent inside and out, there is a short meeting where the supervisors highlight the night experience and we go home, if there is only one show. If there are two shows, we go back to the Cirquador's tent, and wait for the second show and start everything over.

JC always accompanied me to my car in the parking lot when we worked for Cirque. My friend JC is a true gentleman.

Every night is a different experience and my lower back and feet would hurt a lot because we stand the entire time of the show or shows, if there are two. It was an amazing experience and, although I was super tired at the end of the 45 days of the shows, working every day, except Mondays, I was sad that it was time to say goodbye. I wished I could have followed them to the next city!

Now I had to find another job and there I went again to spend all day on the internet, applying from Craigslist and at companies' website. It's just frustrating.

My husband and I took some training to get a permit to work as security in events, which I found okay, because it was kind of what I did as an usher, but I was not excited about it. I didn't want to do that, but yes, I did. What I liked the most about it was that I got to handle a gun in the class and especially in the range, where I could shoot them! I love guns. I'm fascinated by them, but to be honest I think people should not be able to buy a gun so easily. This is a very controversial subject and I won't talk about it. This is my opinion; you can differ and it's all good.

The US Open 2008 started advertising and we both applied; he applied for fun. Because I had the license, we would make a little more money and we both were hired.

My husband was all excited because we would see all the big names in golf and I know this will sound very stupid but I had no clue who Tiger Woods was, or Sergio Garcia or whoever… I just didn't know them. I was not into that sport, plus it was not a very common sport in Brazil. I mean, it probably was for a very select group but I was not interested in it anyway. I used to follow other sports like soccer, volleyball, basketball, and tennis… Anyway, he got his sister excited about it too to work with us and, although she didn't have the license to work as security, she still did the exact same thing as we did.

Before the US Open started, I was called for an interview as Executive Assistant. I couldn't believe it. After seven months of sending my resume, someone finally called for a position that I was looking for! The guy who I will call Bob, for the purpose of giving him a name just so you have a reference because I don't want to keep referring to him as "guy," scheduled an interview and we would meet in a café. That was weird! I was very suspicious, but I did research on the company and it sounded legit and nice so I trusted. After all, we would meet in public anyway, and the place he chose was only a couple of blocks from my house.

The ad had a huge list of tasks that I was going to do if hired and I was up for the challenge, as he was asking for QuickBooks experience. I had no idea what kind of software that was, but I did research and found out it was financial software for invoices… Okay, I've done that with SAP so it might be the same or at least similar.

Among other things, I would have to pack and ship the products and would have to work out of a warehouse twice a week, alone or with another guy. Oh boy, that scared me too.

As I had already made the commitment to work for the US Open, I told that to him on the phone so we wouldn't waste our time. I just didn't want to break a commitment. We set up the interview, as he understood.

On the day of the interview, which was a Friday, I was a little nervous and off I went to the café. I got there and gave a quick look at some people that were already there and didn't think any of them looked like someone looking for an Executive Assistant position. There was a couple at a table outside and a young man in a ponytail and jeans and a shirt, very casual. So I went inside and there was a guy with a laptop on the table.

I picked a table and sat in a way that I could see the door and sidewalk, as the walls of the café were half glass so I could see outside.

I got there around 15 minutes prior to the meeting so I decided to wait inside and watch the people for a minute to see if one of them could be my prospective boss.

Another man arrived and went straight to the guy with the laptop and they started their meeting. They were John and Craig, as I heard the introductions.

Five minutes until the time of my interview and I started to think that the guy in the ponytail was the person I was looking for. Looking more closely, I could see he looked like the picture I saw on the website. He had no beard though and in the website there was no indication in his picture that he had a ponytail but it was him, I was sure. As I was about to go talk to him I guess he had the same thought and before I got up, he did and came inside, coming directly to my table.

He asked if I was Isabel and introduced himself, taking a seat at my table, and we started the interview. He was young and had very nice manners. He was very articulate when speaking and seemed to be very smart and sharp.

I was fascinated by how he was talking about his business. He had this shine of passion for business in his eyes and I could see he was very proud of himself and his business. He was a young and successful man.

The interview was going super easy and our conversation flowed very well. I got a little concerned when he said I would have to be in a not-so-good environment in the storage facility alone with another guy and I would have to work out of his house. Red flags were all around me but somehow I felt that the guy had something about him that I could trust and I really liked him. It was the first time that I hit it off so well with someone in a long time. I had a weird feeling about him, like as if he was my brother. I have no idea why I felt that way about him but it's true. It was a good feeling, a feeling of admiration for a hard-working person.

At the end of the interview, we were pretty relaxed and it seemed to me that we had known each other for a long time. Past lives came to my mind.

When he asked what I thought about everything, asking me if I would be comfortable working with him alone at his house and in a storage facility with another employee, I asked when I would start and he laughed, with a broad and beautiful smile. He said he liked that and told me I was hired if I wanted the position.

I was very surprised and happy. He asked when I could start and my reply to that was, now? He laughed again and he asked if I could start on Monday at 9 am, which he received the yes answer and we said the goodbye thing and did our hand shaking and we went our separate ways.

I was so happy. The salary was not even close to what I was making in Brazil but it would be a start.

On April 14, 2008, I was on my way to my new job, a new career. Actually, I was going back to the career I had when I left Brazil and that made me feel very good and hopeful.

I got to his house and it was a little awkward for me to work at a guy's home but soon I was feeling at home. Bob was an amazing entrepreneur and very intelligent. I admired him a lot and learned a lot from him.

I took note of everything he was telling me and when he went to the part where he taught me how to work with QuickBooks my notes were even more accurate. I actually made a "How To... step by step" which I later handed to him for his next assistant.

We worked together on some orders that he received over the weekend and then we went to the storage facility. I followed him in my truck, as we would not go back to the office, I mean, his house, and after we finished the packaging process we would take the boxes to FedEx. Oh no, that reminds me of my lost package again.

There I met Jeff, his other employee, and again, I'm giving him this name so when I talk about them it will sound better than referring to them as "the guy" and "the assistant."

From the beginning Bob talked to us together and told us, more to address Jeff, that there should be respect between us and that Jeff was going to work under my supervision sometimes, although we would be corroborators and would mainly work together.

I felt bad because Jeff had been working for him longer than I and now, there I was, taking his opportunity to succeed. However, I don't think Jeff seemed to mind. I don't think that even passed through his mind and later, after I tell more about this job, you will understand why I say that.

The three of us worked together and we finished packing the orders around 2 in the afternoon. Jeff and I went to drop them off at FedEx on Encinitas Boulevard, as Bob had an appointment. Oh, and yes, I forgot to mention that I would work part-time only, but I actually liked the idea very much.

On Tuesday my job consisted of processing the new orders from the previous day and filing all the documents that were in a huge pile of papers waiting to be put way. No storage facility work on Tuesdays.

On Wednesday, I went to the office, I mean, his house just to pick up the new orders that he received during the night and from there I went to the storage facility. I was going to work alone with Jeff now.

Bob had told me that Jeff needed to be pushed to do the job or otherwise he would be distracted and wouldn't do the work on time for delivering.

For some reason I felt a deep connection with Jeff that day. It was like I felt the need to help him and even protect him. He was like a child who needed guidance and care. It was a strange feeling but I couldn't help but feel that way towards him. Again, previous life? I always think that way when I have a connection with someone and feel like I've met the person before.

We worked well that day and he told me that Bob was very controlling and that he needed to be in control and feel that he was in control all the time.

I couldn't help but think about the competition between them. It was not really a competition, but more of a sense of power, that both thought they had, where Bob, as per Jeff's perception, had the need to be in control, and Jeff, on his way, knew that Bob felt that way about him. He acted as if he would accept the "submission" and in a certain way would pretend he didn't understand things, and Bob, perceiving Jeff as a good person who needed guidance and a chance, was giving him that chance. I believe Bob felt responsible for Jeff.

It was so weird to be between them. I felt like I had to take sides and I guess I entered in their game, letting Bob believe that I was taking his side and making Jeff believe that I thought he was right. And, to tell the truth, that's really how I felt about it.

It was very nice to be around both. Bob was a very serious yet a very funny young man and we had a lot of fun working together. I met his fiancé, who lived with him, but I almost never saw her there, as she was a pre-school teacher, and would be gone when I arrived for work, and would be back at the end of the day, when I was not there anymore.

The following week, I started working from home. Bob would leave his computer open and I could access it from my house, printing documents and processing orders. And I could create the labels in my house and print them on my printer and Bob would reimburse me for that. That was amazing! I could even stay in my pajamas if I wanted because Steve was not home either!

Every time I worked in the storage facility Jeff would tell me some stories about his life, or would ask me for some advice on how to deal with a girl he was trying to date. I felt like his mother and I guess he saw me as a best buddy. Soon, he started calling me to ask what to do next. It was a little invasive but I didn't care about it because for me he was like a kid and it felt good that someone would look up to me. He always said that he thought I was amazing and that I was right in everything. He was calling me almost every day, sometimes twice or three times, even at night.

I started telling him, he should not call me all the time and he would ask as innocent as a kid, *"Why not? You are my friend! I don't have friends and you are my best friend. I never felt so secure with someone."*

So, what could I say to that? However, I had to put a limit on him but he certainly didn't understand that. Jeff was so innocent, to a point that one day he told me that I was beautiful but that I was not attractive for him or that he was not attracted to me. That could have made me feel terrible but it didn't. I was shocked he would say something like that to a woman and I was not really sure how to take it. But, as I said, he was like a child. He really was a nice big kid but he was a little too much and I told him that. I asked again not to call me all the time, that we could talk when we were at work. He wouldn't stop so I stopped answering his phone calls and he would leave messages, long messages. He was unbelievable. At least he never showed up at my house. I have to give him that.

Time went by very fast and soon June came and as I had talked to Bob even before the interview, I was not going to be able to work from June 12 to 16 because I would work for the US Open.

The US Open took place from June 12 to 16 of 2008 at Torrey Pines, La Jolla. Our supervisor was amazing.

So there I was working side by side with my husband. The first day I worked in the main entrance, screening people's purses, bags, pockets. No cell phones were allowed and some people would be all upset that they needed to go back to the car or hotel. They would beg me, saying they would keep it shut, but rules were rules and we couldn't let them in.

I caught at least three people trying to be smart asses as they were throwing their cell phones through the fences to friends or simply in the ground and, because I could not leave my post, I would radio and give the description of the patron(s) and where he/they headed. Soon, they would be escorted back to my gate, all upset and arguing with the security or police officer that was taking them away.

My husband would come home all excited talking about the famous players but that wouldn't ring any bells on me.

THE AMERICAN DREAM AND EVERYTHING IN BETWEEN

The last day I was working again with my husband in the 18th hole, which I had no idea what that meant. My sister-in-law worked in the players' locker room and she would see them all and their families all the time. She, like my husband, was very excited. I was exhausted by the end of the last day. I would work from 8:00 am to 8:00 pm and some days from 10:00 am to 10:00 pm. Standing all day in the sun was not something that I could be excited about and by the end of the last day all I wanted was for the event to end. My feet were hurting a lot, just like they did when I worked for Cirque du Soleil. My supervisor asked if I could work a couple more days and, as I had my other job lined up, I had to turn him down, but I was glad I didn't have to stay and work standing for one more day. Plus, I really didn't like doing that job. I mean, it was okay, but that was not what I had in mind. Working for a couple of days in events like that is fun but I'd rather do something else.

At the end I was more familiar with the game and players and I actually started liking it, and today I enjoy watching it on TV. And yes, I know who Tiger Woods is. I like Phil!

I went back to my normal days of work with Bob, Jeff, storage and home. Now, I was working more hours because when you work from home, you can't control yourself and check emails and receive phone calls. Bob started calling me late at night or on my non-working hours and weekends. I didn't mind but my husband started to get upset. He would say that Bob was using me, and I was letting him do it and we would argue because of that. I knew he was right but I didn't want to lose that job. I liked working with Bob, even though it was not exactly what I wanted to do for the rest of my life.

I would complain to my husband, as that was the only job I found and it was not what the title meant to be. I was not doing any Executive Assistant work, but more like an Administrative Assistant or Office Assistant for that matter, which was okay. Although I loved to work not having to dress up for work, I had to admit that I was tired of carrying heavy boxes and getting all dirty because of the newspaper we used to wrap the products, every other day. Some of the boxes were very heavy, especially when we had to do inventory counting and move the boxes around. It was frustrating and my back didn't appreciate that much, but I liked working with Bob and Jeff.

At the end of June, Bob and I had a meeting and he wanted to fill me in on a fair that he would be working in LA in September. He asked me to go but I would have to spend the two nights in LA with him and Jeff. I brought the subject to Steve and he said no way and he would say that the "guy" was just using me because he wanted me to transport the products in my truck. We discussed it but I had to agree with him because I thought he was probably right and I understood that business was business. But with Steve not wanting me to go I had to tell Bob that I couldn't go.

He was not happy and I was not comfortable. I thought I should go with him. He was a very nice guy and of course he would pay for gas and everything.

Something changed after I said I couldn't go and, understandably, he started treating me very differently. He would answer my questions in a rude way, or snap at me or he would tell me to do my job instead of asking him about things all the time and I was not even asking him questions all the time. He was just very upset with me.

One day he called me around 6:30 pm. I was preparing dinner so I had my phone in the ear and at the same time was stirring something on the stove. I guess I could have told him I would call him back but I didn't do that. The phone call was not good and it was cutting his words and when I asked him to repeat something and again he snap something back at me, and I just couldn't take that anymore.

I replied back in the same tone that he used and told him how I was feeling. He said I couldn't handle a stressful situation and our conversation turned into a huge argument and I told him I was quitting. He said fine and hung up the phone.

I was so upset. I was crying after he hung up on me and I turned off the stove and cried and cried. Why was that happening? It was like a nightmare. Here I was, trying to do my best, working after hours and I was not even an employee. I was a contractor under 1099 and because I couldn't go to LA for the fair, this man, which I liked and really respected for being a super talented entrepreneur, was disrespecting me and not treating me well.

He called me back and I didn't answer the phone. I was too upset with him. He left a message apologizing and said he would call me again for me to please, pick up the phone.

He called back five minutes later and I answered the phone. He said that I was right. That he realized he was treating me different and that it was because I didn't want to help him when he needed me the most.

I told him that this was not a good situation and that I didn't think I could work with him anymore. He asked me if I could stay until the fair was over and I agreed of course.

Next morning I went to work but it was a very heavy environment. I felt bad because I liked him a lot and wanted to work with him but at the same time my pride was talking louder than anything else. I always had this thing in me. If I thought that I was not being treated right, it was hard for me to forget. I call that childish but I can't change it either.

That day, I gave him all the work I had done and, without being asked for it, the "How To…" that I had made when I started. I figured he could give it to anybody with no experience and that they would do the job without his help.

He checked it out and said that that was amazing and asked me to reconsider and continue working for him. I said no again and boy I regretted that at the moment I said it, but for pride or childishness I didn't change my mind! I really wish I did.

They had the fair and I worked from my house and storage alone the three days that they were gone.

I went to work on the following Monday and it would be my last day. We worked all day together, and my heart was heavy and I was very sad. He was sad too and I could see that. At the end of the day he told me if I changed my mind, I would have my job at any time.

Jeff and I remained friends. He would continue calling me when he needed advice for his girlfriend encounters and he would say that he missed me.

There I was, out of a job again due to stupidity and childishness. I knew that it would not look good on my resume the short five months working as Executive Assistant. Even if I thought I did the right thing, which I really didn't think it was right, it would still look bad in my resume but no matter what, I would tell the truth in my interviews… that is, if I had another chance.

So, I started my saga of internet job searching again, spending hours filling out applications and sending out resumes through Craigslist.

I left my job at the end of September and in October I found a job at a big department store. I would work as a cashier and it was part-time, and again, temporary. They were hiring because of the holidays that were approaching. The salary was even lower than what I was paid by the agency when I worked for Cirque du Soleil and, of course, Bob.

This was so frustrating but I had to give it a try. The hours of work were terrible. One day I would work from 7:00 am to 1:00 pm, the next day it would be from 2:00 pm to 10:00 pm, the next from 9:00 am to 3:00 pm and all kinds of different schedules so I could not have gotten a second job even if I had wanted to.

When I told Steve I was going to accept that job he told me I didn't need to work but if I wanted to, I should focus on something that I liked to do. He always supported me and this is why I was able to stay out of work and not worry about bills or anything but, as I was used to work and always provided for myself, I couldn't just sit home and live as if I was a princess. That was not me. I could never use someone like that. At least that's how I would feel, that I was using him, if I did that.

So I took the job and it was okay, but I felt that I was almost paying to work. If I made $9.00/hour and I would work four or six hours and I would spend about $5 or $10 in gas everyday…how much I was making after the discounts of the taxes? I hated to think about that.

I liked when they sent me to work on the floor, which meant that I had to go to a certain section and get products from a different section that people left there when they decided they didn't want to buy it anymore. They would just leave the product wherever they feel like, and we would

63

pick them up and take them back to the front for another employee to sort them out, and take them back to the right section.

At the end of the second week I was sure I didn't want to do that anymore. I couldn't see myself getting anywhere doing that and, besides, I was just not happy; in fact, I was so unhappy that I would cry on my way to work. I never told anybody about this but then, after another couple of weeks I quit and this time I didn't regret it. My feet loved that I did that too because they were too tired to stand and walk so many hours, carrying me around!

Back to Craigslist! Damn, I was tired of this whole thing. If I was not married, I would certainly go back to Brazil!!
I started taking English classes in Old Town but I thought it was not helping much. I had to go to another school because I didn't think that one had much to offer me. It was okay to go and spend three or four hours talking to people from all over the world but most of Brazilians wanted to speak Portuguese on the break and I wanted to speak English; there was a rule about not speaking in your own language but people didn't care or maybe I'm too serious about rules. The rules were not really my point here. The fact is that I was here so I wanted to speak the language to improve my English skills and if I'm paying for something, I want to get the most of it.

I found another temporary job. This lady had a dating site and we were supposed to help her organize her paperwork. We spent one week separating her papers into piles at a storage facility in San Diego. Again the money against the gas was something I couldn't get over. But I liked her a lot. She was a nice lady. She hired two other girls to work with us and we had good time.

The week was over and so was the job. Back to Craigslist and all the companies' websites but then I would have a break because we would travel to Alaska! Another cruise! In fact, we went there twice, one time in the winter and another in the summer, both of which I only have great things to say about.

This flexibility was something I really liked and started to get used to. Steve, like me, loves to travel and he had all these hours that he could take off anytime. It was somehow working out very well but Steve, because he could take off anytime he wanted, would ask me to travel when I was working and I would say I couldn't. Like when I was working for Bob, he wanted me to take a week off and I was like, "how can I take off like that? I just started working." But he would say that I was not an employee and I could take off anytime I wanted. That I was taking things too seriously and, besides, I didn't need to work.

That was his excuse and I couldn't believe how he would think like that. I guess I was way too responsible. But that's how I was raised and because in Brazil I had vacation once a year, that's when I used to travel around and of course on the weekends. I always loved to travel.

When we came back from the trip, we met a Brazilian girl who used to work one block away from my house at an Italian restaurant, which, by the way, is a tiny place with very good food.

I asked her how she got the job and she told me that she lied to the owner in the interview, saying that she used to work for McDonald's in Brazil, and that's what everybody does when they go to work in a restaurant because they will not call Brazil to check your employment history.

So I found out that day why I was never called for an interview in a restaurant…that's why I could not find a job as a waitress because I never mentioned that I had that type of experience before. Smart.

Although I always sent my resume to restaurants, I was not really looking forward to getting a job as a waitress. I still wanted to find a job in my area of expertise. I wish I did not have that pride in me and I wish I would call Bob and how I wish he would call me back, which, of course, none of us ever did. Perhaps we both had too much pride. Well, that was me, because he had asked me twice to reconsider. In fact, that from my part and perspective was just pure stupidity.

I found another part-time job to work at Hilton Hotel near Del Mar Fairgrounds for a show car company that would showcase in Del Mar and my job was to stuff bags and give them away. The bags were filled with marketing materials, business cards, flyers, etc. Two days of work. At least it was a work that I could do seated! I'm starting to think that I'm a spoiled brat!

Another job like that came up. This time I was going to work for four days at Del Mar Fairgrounds working as Sales Associate in a huge fair. I hate sales, but I was up for the job and I enjoyed doing it. We didn't have to go push someone to buy something; we just had to be there for them if they had any question, which I liked much better.

That job was over soon too and I was back to my frantic job search. Searching for jobs all day makes you very tired. My neck and back were very sore at the end of the day.

One day Jeff called me and told me a friend of his was looking for a person to help him with his orders and he wanted to know if I was interested and I told him I was so he called the guy and told him about me, and the guy asked him to ask me to call him.

I gave him a call and, for the love of God, I couldn't understand him. He was an English man and his accent was very thick. We scheduled a time at his house, which was where I was going to work if I got the job.

This is very interesting. He gave me the name of the company and it took me a while to figure out which company it was because I couldn't understand his accent and of course I didn't want to ask him to repeat it over and over. I spent some time on the website trying to find his company. I finally found it, after typing all kinds of similar names that sounded like what he said and that's probably the reason people didn't want to hire me and it's totally understandable now. I checked his website and found out he, among many other things, sold religious stuff.

There I went again, all dressed up for the interview. He was in blue jeans and sandals. I love this relaxed environment of these home offices here. He was a tall guy, laid-back type and I liked him a lot. The interview went well. Well, I should say our chat went well. He was an interesting man and explained his business and what he expected from me.

Guess what? He told me he was concerned that his clients would not understand me over the phone because of my accent. What? He had an accent too and I couldn't understand him either! I thought he seemed to read my mind and he said, *"I know, that sounds stupid. I have an accent too but the difference between us is that my first language is English."*

I felt a little uncomfortable and I knew he was right, which didn't really make sense to me because I was absolutely sure that I had the skills and all it would take to do any job if given a chance, but life goes on and we have to live with it, adapting. I'm a Brazilian and I have an accent so I have to deal with it. Many times, when I talk to people, it's funny because they turn their ears to me as if to understand what I'm saying... then they repeat EXACTLY what I just said! So I believe.

Anyway, he showed me around and introduced me to his assistant, as I would be working with him. His assistant would receive the orders and give them to me to separate and hand them back to him so he could finish processing them. We would be doing together what I used to do alone when I worked for Bob. I guess Craig gave me the job because he wanted to help me out.

I would work on a needed basis, which means that it was not even part-time... just when they needed me but I accepted the offer.

There I met a very nice lady, in her late 30s or early 40s. She designs websites and was working on Craig's websites. Again, I'm calling him Craig but this is not his name.

I got along very well with the two people who were working at his office. Sometimes I would be disgusted because I would touch rat urine when I was picking up the products in this shed Craig had in the yard, where he stored a lot of the products and it was upsetting to me and of course I would compare it with the jobs I had in Brazil. I was making less than half of what I was making there, and doing things that I never dreamt of doing. Not in a good way, but I guess I should be thankful for the opportunities I had.

Although I really liked Craig, who was a super nice and laid-back gentleman, I was not happy with my situation here and I had tried everything. I was tired, frustrated and disappointed and I missed my family, friends and my dear dog, which I had to give to someone else because he bit my mom a couple of times.

It was not his fault because I knew she provoked him, but she was my mom and I didn't want him to hurt her. I couldn't bring him here and I regret that so much, as I gave him away instead of fighting for him.

67

Before I gave him to someone else I asked my siblings if they could keep him for me but didn't have any luck with that. To this day I keep trying to find the person I gave him to so I could get him back but I never found the woman. Supposedly, she moved to the Northeast of Brazil and nobody knew any other information about her. I still cry for him and I hope he is doing well and that they treat him good. I love my Willy! And boy I miss him!!!

This is one thing I regret in my life and I will never forgive myself for that. I know I should move on but I simply can't.

One day my husband asked me if I wanted to apply to work for the LA County and I did. I took the test online and the results came in the mail. I was placed in the eligible list. Needless to say, they never called me to offer a job.

So I applied to the San Diego County as well and took the test. Guess what? I was also placed in the eligible list too but again, they never called. What is up with that? They place you on an eligible list and never call you for the job.

I tried pretty much every company in San Diego County and even Irvine and surrounding areas. Nothing happened. No interviews, no phone calls.

I was tired and one day I was talking to a neighbor and asked him if he knew of someone that needed help and he said that he didn't know and that he had someone working for him but he would let me know if he knew something. David was a weird guy who lived below my apartment in Encinitas. A few days later, he knocked on my door and asked me if I was still looking for work and I said yes. He told me what he did and asked if I wanted to help him he would be happy to hire me. Not really hire me; I would work under a contractor's agreement. He also told me that he wouldn't need me all the time; in fact, he would need me three or four days every other month, depending on the demand of his products.

Job description: separate orders, pack and ship. He worked selling aviation publications and, as he explained to me later, the airports change things all the time so the pilots need to buy the maps with the new routes for various airports and that's how he had been in business for quite some time. He told me it pays the bills.

68

David was a weird but an interesting man. We talked a lot in the beginning but he would get distracted a lot and make many mistakes with the invoices while we were talking so we started talking only when we were packing.

He lived in many places, including Hawaii and Mexico, and did many different things. He worked in all kinds of jobs until he started working with aviation publications.

In the past, he had been a part of a motorcycle club and the only thing he kept from that time was his ponytail.

He lived right below my house, which for me was great! All I had to do was jump from the second floor and land right in front of his front door. Well, I never really did that; I preferred to come down the stairs.

His house was so dark and we worked with the door opened, thank God! He had a few pieces of furniture and artwork that he cherished because they belonged to his mother and he kept them when she passed way. He told me he could never get rid of them because they were the only things from her and looking at them every day made him feel his mother's presence.

I was getting the feeling that everybody in America works from home, which I found very cool. Maybe I should have a business like that on my own and many things came to mind on what kind of business I could open myself. I thought of selling Brazil's products, like bikinis, sandals, coasters, chocolate...

I even thought of picking up all those, unwanted piece for furniture and other stuff people leave on the street, in front of their houses, to sell them myself. Think about it, I had nothing to lose and now that I'm writing about it, maybe it would have been a great idea!

But I never really deepened the thoughts about any of the business ideas I had because I really don't like sales and I don't see myself as a salesperson, so I kept working with David and Craig and whatever other little job I could find in the events field.

When I say that to people, I mean, that I don't like sales and they know I have a degree in Marketing they say, *"But why did you graduate in Marketing, then?"*

I agree that Marketing is a tool for sales but it's not really sales as I think about it. I don't have to talk to people to try to convince them to buy my products or services, for that matter. Marketing is the tool to facilitate the sales process. Well, it's like sales but it's different, if you know what I mean.

Meanwhile, I kept sending my resume to all kinds of organizations and every job post from Craigslist or LinkedIn I thought it would fit. In doing that, I got another job interview so there I went again. The job was in Del Mar. It was for the role of Administrative Assistant. The owner was very nice and we had a nice talk but he was concerned because he thought I would not stay for a long time because for him I was overqualified for the job. He didn't even care about my accent. He said he understood me well and that his clients would get used to it, once they knew me.

You gotta be kidding me! I tried to convince him that all I wanted was an opportunity to show I could contribute to the growth of the company. It didn't work. He said that he preferred to have someone that was starting their career, a college girl or boy perhaps. And he didn't even know about my quitting jobs, as I didn't put that in my resume.

Great, now I had a problem with being overqualified. I was really tired of applying for all kinds of jobs and making changes in my resume. I had all kinds of resumes by then.

One day I went for an interview, again in a café. This time it was with a girl in her late 20s. It was for a Personal Assistant. The salary was good and I would have to be a kind of governance of a house in Rancho Santa Fe, a very nice neighborhood. I would have to cook for the family. I guess I didn't get that job because I was not a cook or because I didn't have experience in managing someone else's house.

Another time I went for a babysitter position and I really liked the child and her mother. Tracy looked like a model from a magazine. Tall, blonde, slim. She really looked like a model. She had a business and worked from home, and she needed someone to take care of her eight-month-old baby girl.

The girl, named Tammy, was an adorable, happy and chubby child. My goodness, she was so heavy!

Well, I guess she wanted someone who had more experience with kids. Having nieces and nephews and watching them didn't have what it takes to be a babysitter.

That's pretty bad, not being able to get a babysitting job!

CHAPTER SEVEN

Volunteer Work

I start volunteering at ECERT, which stands for Encinitas Community Emergency Response Team. They prepare you to help in case a disaster occurs. They train you at a fire station with firefighters, of course. CPR is one of the things you learn in the trainings they have throughout the year. It's a great way to learn, meet people and who knows what opportunities can come up from volunteering? It can open doors. And from this volunteer work I had the most amazing opportunity of my life. I'll tell you all about it later. A hint: it has to do with TV.

In 2008, I moved from Encinitas to Carlsbad and would still drive to Encinitas to work for both guys and kept sending my resume and applying for every single job I thought I would fit in. Full- or part-time, it didn't matter.

I had an application with some staffing companies but no luck with them either, except for the events.

One day I got a call from one of the staffing companies and it was for a position of Executive Assistant. She sent me all the information on the company, the job description and she told me that she thought I was a great fit. We set up an interview and off I went.

I met the HR Manager and, after a quick talk, she said she would send in another person to interview me and after she left the room, the HR Director came to talk to me. The interview went well, in my point of view. He seemed to understand everything I was saying and he asked me to wait to see if the executive I was going to work with was available. He said he liked me but it was not up to him to decide, as I was going to work with someone else. Sounded very good and there was I in the room, a little nervous and excited at the same time. So far, I had spoken to two people for the job and it sounded like I was doing good, as I was now getting the chance to speak with the executive I was going to work with, if everything went well. It was my opportunity to work with a great company and the salary was great. For the first time since I moved to California, I was almost getting what I believed I was meant to and, most importantly, would be doing what I liked doing and as a bonus as it was only about five minutes from my house.

An elegant gentleman knocked at the door and entered the room and I stood up. We greeted each other with a firm handshake and eye contact. I had a great feeling about him. I had no idea what he was thinking. We talked a lot. We laughed at times, we were serious at times. I felt confident and I was happy, then he said, *"Isabel, I really enjoyed talking with you. I have no doubt that you are an amazing professional. Your resume is terrific and your English is very good and I'm convicted that you have all that takes to be a great Executive Assistant but I can't hire you. I'm sorry. I'm concerned that my clients will not understand you over the phone and you would be in contact with them about eighty percent of the time and I don't think that will work, unfortunately."*

I said in my most dignified way, *"I understand, and I've heard that before, but if given a chance, I believe you would be happy and your clients would get used to my accent and I would also improve my English skills. I could work on accent reduction."*

Then he said, *"Look, I know that this is difficult, but do not give up. I'm sure that you will find a great job. You have everything that takes so keep trying and don't give up."*

Well, that was nice to say, right? Sure, how is that going to happen if nobody gives me an opportunity? You are not in my shoes! I wanted to say that to him but it was not his fault. He had the right to choose what or who would be a better fit for his company. It was clearly not me.

There was nothing else I could say. I was feeling defeated, humiliated and extremely sad so I put a nice smile in my face, thanked him for his time and told him I enjoyed talking to him and that it was nice to meet him.

We stood up and shook hands with the eye contact. This time I saw pain in his eyes. It was probably the reflex of my own feelings. My own pain reflected in his eyes.

He opened the door and we said good luck to each other and I left without looking back. I don't know how I was looking when I passed by the reception but I gave a weak smile to the girl behind the table and left the office, wishing her a great day. When I closed the door of the office behind me, tears ran down my face like a furious river and when I got to the car I had no strength to leave so I stayed there, in the car crying and feeling like the worst person in the world, the most stupid one on earth. I wished I had someone to hug and to tell me everything would be okay, that I would find something better; that they were the ones who lost.

But as I said, life goes on and I started breathing and thinking of good times, thinking of my Willy until I was able to smile again. Willy was my dog that I left in Brazil and I regret that to this day, remember? I breathed deeply a couple of times, wiped the tears off of my face and went back home.

Now, this was the third time I had been told that I wouldn't get a better job because of my accent. Well, they didn't say that, what they said is that they couldn't hire me because their clients would not understand me, which for me, is exactly the same thing.

I couldn't believe this and I kept thinking to myself, if that was true how about Sofia Vergara or Penelope Cruz?

I mentioned that about them just to break the seriousness of the subject but I was always thinking about a couple of people I met that I could barely understand what they were saying because of their accent and seemed they didn't have a problem finding a job, did they? I can't tell, as I'm not in their shoes either. I know nothing about their lives. We can't judge anybody, never.

Talking about accents, I have to share a frustrating incident that happened to me many times when I called my doctor to schedule an appointment. Here is how the conversation always developed:

Attendant: *"Name of the establishment, this is (her name), how can I help you?"*

Me: *"Hi, this is Isabel Canzoneri and I would like to schedule an appointment with Dr. ..."*

Attendant: *"Sure, what is your date of birth?"*

Me: *"December 20, 19..."* (oh, come on, you didn't think I would tell you that right?)

Attendant: *"Okay, so what is the problem?"*

Me: *"...."* I would say and she...

Attendant: *"Can you repeat that, please?"* and I repeated.

Attendant: *"Sorry, the line is cutting, I can't understand you. Can you repeat?"*

And that would go on and on and on every single time I would call, either to schedule an appointment for myself or for my husband.

One day I was so tired of her that when she got to the part that she would say, *"Sorry, the line is cutting and I can't understand you..."* I cut her off and said, *"Listen, lady, every time I call to schedule an appointment or to ask for a prescription, return a call to a doctor or a nurse, the same thing happens and I don't know how many times I've called you. The line is not cutting. You said that because you don't understand what I'm saying or you don't want to understand and I understand it's because of my accent. But listen, you have an accent as well and it's not easy for me to understand what you say, but I do my best. Perhaps with a little more willingness on your part, you would be able to understand everybody that calls the office."*

Attendant: *"I'm sorry, the problem is really that we are having problems with the line and the phones and..."*

I interrupted her again, I know it was rude but I was really tired of her same old same phrase. I said, *"You don't need to say that anymore and I will tell you something. Just ask my doctor or his nurse to call me back, please."*

And I was polite enough to say "please."

Attendant: *"That's okay, I can schedule you for..."* She gave me the date and time for the appointment. Was that difficult?

Me: *"Thank you and have a great day."*

Attendant: *"Thank you, you too, and I'm sorry."*

We hung up and that never happened again. She would understand me every time, the first time she asked after that.

Until today I wonder if she really understood me or was just afraid of my outburst but I didn't care; it didn't bother me anymore.

It's funny how some people have the power to push our buttons but, on the other hand, I believe it's up to us to control these thoughts and feelings. And the push our buttons thing is just our own weakness. We allow the outside environment to disrupt our structure and affect us.

In a moment of weakness I decided that I was not going to look for a job anymore. I guess I felt defeated, really. I wanted to go back to my country, where I would be given the opportunity to go back to what I knew well what to do, be an Executive Assistant or Event Coordinator and would have a great salary. Even better salary than when I left because they would value me more just for living abroad. Isn't that funny?

Every time things like this happened to me, I would write to my dear and best friends and sometimes to my brother in Brazil. They were my support from the moment they heard I was getting married and staying in the US until now. I have few but great best friends in Brazil.

I didn't have any friends here, as you can imagine. It's not easy to make friends here. People are different, or better put, we are strangers in a different world so we are the different ones. It's another culture and to me, Americans, well maybe not all of them, and forgive me if I offend

76

anybody, are all very private people, which I don't think it's a bad thing, on the contrary, I love it but sometimes it's a bit too much for me. I didn't feel welcomed as our people in Brazil would make anyone feel if they were to move to that country.

I understand and there's nothing wrong with that. It's cultural, and to tell you the truth I like it. I think sometimes Brazilians can be very invasive. They don't set boundaries and it's a problem sometimes or perhaps a lot of times. Truth to be told, all the time!

Well, about friends, I'm lying. I do have friends here and they are the type of friends that you would die for. I'm talking about my two great best friends and they are my beautiful and lovely parents-in-law, Pat and Nick. We are always together and every single time I have the pleasure to have them with me, my life is so much better. We laugh a lot together. We have this date every Wednesday and I couldn't be happier. When we can't make it that day we do it at another day, most likely Thursdays. They made my life so much easier and better and made me feel very welcomed from the beginning. I have no words to thank them enough. I absolutely love them both and I'm not just saying this because they might read this book; it's the ultimate truth.

I talked to them about some issues I had here too but I didn't want to be whining and whining all the time about my problems trying to find jobs with them.

Nick used to tell me I have to slow down when I speak because sometimes people would not understand me because I do speak too fast. So, sometimes I would speak really slowly with him and he would say with the same slowness, *"See, there you go, I can understand you perfectly"* and we would laugh. He said I had to speak slowly because American people are slow. More laughs. Hey, he said that, not me.

They were always telling me that I should apply for citizenship and I would say I would do that. They kept pushing me to do that and would say that maybe it would be a way for me to be hired more easily.

Time goes by fast when you are spending all day on the internet searching for jobs, filling up applications, sending resumes…it's like having a job, working hard all day. Actually it's more than that, because you are doing all that hard work and you are not being compensated for it. It's like volunteer work without the satisfaction. Let's just put it that way.

I know that it sounds negative, but how can you be positive if all your attempts to find a job fail?

You are probably thinking, *Why didn't she go back to school?*

I thought of doing that many times, but there are a couple of reasons for me not doing that. The first one is that, as I said before, I hate depending on someone else to pay for my things and that's because my whole life I had to provide for myself, as my family couldn't afford to help me. On the contrary, the members of my family would need to work hard and take care of providing the basic needs for the maintenance of the house, like groceries, rent, utility bills, etc. You know, share the bills and responsibilities.

As I said, my family was not rich so each one of the family members would have to help both at the house and pay for our own expenses and invest in training if we wanted to succeed, and that's how my brother and I got to graduate. We paid for our own college and whatever other training we needed, like English, Spanish, computer training, etc.

The thing is, I hated the fact that I would have to ask for money from my husband to pay for my education here. I know it doesn't sound right, as that's what husbands and wives are for, to support each other, but I couldn't take it. I was afraid one day I would hear something like, "*If you are in this position now it's because I helped you*" and I just could not accept that.

My poor husband must be mad at me reading this now, but I'm not going to lie that, that passed through my mind a lot then. Sorry, baby, I didn't mean to hurt you and I apologize if I did. I thank you for your support and deep inside I knew you would never do that to me, but my fear and my pride were bigger.

Anyway, the second issue I had with that was going back to college! See, I had to work all day and go to school at night. It was not easy and very tiring. I had to get up 5 or 5:30 in the morning, take a bus and or the train to get to work, a commute of 1 to sometimes 2 hours and a half, and work all day, from 8 to 5 or 9 to 6 and go straight to school, meaning that, most of the time, I would not eat until I was back home around midnight, because I didn't have money to buy a sandwich or snack. That was my everyday routine for four years!

That's how I and most of the people who live in Brazil get through college.

In the previous years during high school and earlier, I used to work closer to home. Since 5th grade, I had gone to school from 7:00 pm to 10:30 pm because I had to work during the day...

On the weekends, there was no rest. We needed to study for tests, do homework. Now imagine you do all that, you work your ass off, day and night and then you move to another country and the opportunities you have are to work in a job that will not pay half of what you used to make in your country and yet, you couldn't find that job! It's hard, isn't it?

I did find another couple of jobs after that. One was to work for a week and help this nice lady go through her paperwork and file it all.

Our job was to separate all the papers in piles of alike documents. This lady had this dating website. It was very nice to work with her and I met a couple of girls. I still have them on my professional network but we don't really talk and perhaps one of the reasons is our age difference. I could be their mother.

Then I worked for another lady and I basically had to help her organize paperwork as well and help her with light cleaning. I did that a couple of times. She is also a nice lady and I still have her in both my personal and professional networks.

Then I worked for Cirque du Soleil again in 2010, at the beginning of the year. I guess I don't need to describe everything again. It was one month and a half and I loved it!

In March after the Cirque du Soleil ended, I found another job similar to it. I was going to work as Event Ambassador for the San Diego County Fair, same site as Cirque du Soleil at Del Mar Fairgrounds.

My task was to give information to patrons, direct them sometimes, and take them to their seats. Easy job, really, and I worked for them for three years, 2010, 2011 and 2012. Summer jobs, to be more specific. I still have some connections there.

The first year I had a couple of problems with two other colleagues, as they wanted to impose on us a new in the job because they had been doing that for three or four years. One was a girl who later I became friends with; not friends like Brazil, but we got along well after things were put in black and white. I don't take insults from anybody and I say what I think to you...not to someone else...so we talked.

The guy was a little difficult and I don't know why; I just couldn't swallow him. Maybe I was the difficult one, who knows? Psychology would say that it's like a mirror...you don't like in people what you don't like in yourself...maybe it's true...but I could never like him and for the next years that I worked with him again, I just tried to avoid him at all costs and I succeeded in doing just that. I would stay away from him and anytime he would approach a group I was with, I would leave. It's terrible, I know, but I can't change that. And it's not that I didn't try. I did, but it didn't work; it was stronger than me and I can't explain either. I'm very honest and if I don't like someone, for no reason, sometimes, I can't even talk to them. Maybe one day I will be able to explain that or change...maybe. I really hope I will.

While I was working with aviation publications and another company selling religious items, I was also working with events, big or small, such as Cirque du Soleil, San Diego County Fair, US Open Golf. I worked everywhere I could. Usually they were temporary jobs related to events, which I liked and which were during the summer.

I started to like the freedom I had having this type of job and I was able to travel in between these assignments whenever my husband wanted to take off on a vacation. Of course I could only afford that because I was married because the money I was making would not cover all the expenses related to that. To travel, I mean.

Despite everything, I consider myself very lucky! At the end of 2010, an opportunity to work as Property Manager where I was living in Carlsbad knocked on my door, literally.

At the end of November, I was on the internet in my dining room searching the internet, guess for what? Jobs, of course, and from the dining area I could see the entire street coming down as my house was in the bottom of the street so I saw two gentlemen, coming down the road and leaving notes on all the tenants' doors. They were not ringing the bell or knocking on the doors; they simply placed an envelope on the floor in front of the door. They didn't look like them but I thought they were those religious people who knock on our doors to preach us.

After they left, I got the envelope they left, half under my mat, and when I read it I couldn't have felt happier. They were looking for someone to be the manager for the place. This facility had 24 units and I had no idea what a Property Manager did; well, I had an idea but never looked into it.

I checked my resume, made some changes in it to fit the position, and prepared a cover letter.

When I wrote the email, I stated that I had applied for the position before, in 2008, to be more specific. But another person was chosen at that time, and I hoped this time I would have an opportunity to talk to them in person, and hopefully, after the meeting, show them what values I could bring to the table with my experience.

To tell the truth, I was not so confident but I wanted the job. I wanted to prove to myself that if I didn't give up I could have a chance and if I was persistent, there would be no doubt that, sooner or later, I would have the opportunity I was waiting for.

In my mind, nothing had changed since I applied for the first time in 2008 when a negative response came in form of email reply. That thought almost made me to give up but I hit the send key on my computer's keyboard and said a silent prayer. I had hope besides against all odds.

On the following morning, I received an email from the owners, which I was afraid to open. So I didn't open it right away because I was not prepared to read I was not selected due to my Brazilian background. I went out to run some errands and when I came back, I thought I was prepared for whatever they had to say and I opened it.

They informed me in the email that they received a couple of applications and they were going to set up interviews with the candidates, and they would like to set up an appointment for us to meet. Furthermore, they explained a little bit about the scope of work and wanted to know if the following day at noon would work for me.

I could not believe it. I had an interview with the two owners. I didn't know if that was good or bad. Having an interview with one person was scary enough, let alone two!

I answered the email, thanking them for the opportunity they were giving me to meet them and agreeing with the time they suggested. I couldn't play hard to get at any point in my journey to find a decent job here.

As soon as I sent the email I went to their website and was surprised to find out that they were not only regular rentals. They had a few units that they offered fully furnished which were accessible homes for people with a spinal cord injury. These were for people who would come from all over the world seeking therapy in the neighborhood in the hopes to walk again after they had a serious accident, which left them paralyzed from the neck or waist down.

I spent the entire afternoon on their website. I also went to the website of the organization that provided the treatment for those people with SCI. I learned a lot from both websites and at the end of the day I was feeling confident again that I would get the job. The interview would be in my house.

I woke up that morning and straightened the house and printed my resume and a list of questions I had for them about the business.

Everything was ready. My husband was home, as he didn't work on certain days of the week. He would be helping in the job, as they were looking for a couple to run the place so I thought he should participate in the meeting.

They arrived and we sat on the couch in the living room. We introduced ourselves and…oh Lord, one of the guys had a very heavy accent from someplace in Europe, which I recognized as England because he was very proper and they were punctual. Great, we both had accents…the difference, though, was that his primary language was English and that was my second language. Here comes the challenge. I've heard that before, not one, but many times.

They were very proper and elegant. Although they were well-dressed they were not fancy-dressed. They were quite different from one another, in everything I could think of. One was probably my age and the other one probably a little older than my husband, so I thought.

I thanked them for the opportunity to meet them and the interview had officially started.

I asked them if they needed my resume and the English man, whose name was Patrick, said they had it and went straight to the point saying that they had a couple of experiences with two different managers but things didn't work quite well and that was the reason they were looking for someone else.

From the beginning, the older gentleman, the English man, talked more than the younger. The younger was on the phone, texting, emailing or whatever he was doing most of the time and would participate only when asked for confirmation or information from his partner.

I thought that was annoying and I was thinking, *"what kind of person is this? Why is he here if he doesn't even look at me? Is the older man his lover and is he just coming along as a companion?"* I had to forget about him and concentrate on the interview. This was none of my business anyway. *What's wrong with me? Come on, Isabel, focus!*

Patrick, the English man, went ahead telling me the reasons things were not working out and I was shocked by some facts he exposed to me about previous management.

The same way I had problems understanding his English accent in the beginning, seems that he was also having a hard time understanding me. Here we go again! But within ten minutes of meeting we were all very comfortable and understanding each other better.

Patrick asked if I had any questions about the company or about the job and when I started talking about it, he seemed to be impressed. No, he seemed to be very impressed. Score!

I told them I had been living there for more than a year and I had no idea that they offered such great services to people from all over the world. That their facilities had what the competitors didn't have and that it was a huge plus for them.

At that point, even the younger man on the phone, Romeo I'm going to call him, stopped doing whatever he was doing and looked at me with more interest. I was feeling very proud of my research.

Well, I got his attention, and that was pretty darn good. I didn't spend my entire afternoon searching their website, the other place's website and even their competitors for nothing. I wanted the job and I wanted to prove that I was capable of doing it.

I talked a lot about their organization and business and I showed them that I understood their business and my husband, who was not into the meeting either because he was paying more attention to our cat, which was rubbing one of the guys' legs, the English gentleman, at this point told them that I was a very smart and competent.

Go back a little, please. Can you picture that? Can you picture a cat rubbing the legs of an English gentleman during a job interview? I don't think he was appreciating that love and attention from our kitty.

My husband was more like being my support and he made it clear by telling them that he would not be involved in the day-by-day business management but would help to patrol the property or whatever I needed.

The conversation turned around and Patrick asked me to talk about my experience in Brazil.

I told them that I used to work for multinational corporations as Executive Assistant and earlier as Event Coordinator and that in both cases I had to supervise the services of Receptionists, Administrative Assistants, Security Guards, Maintenance and Cleaning crew.

Patrick asked me where I had learned English and I told them I went to school and then, when I started working for the multinational companies, they paid for it and he said that my English was very good and that it was way better than his Portuguese.

I didn't find his joke funny because that was the main issue I had been facing trying to find a job in the same area I was working when I was in Brazil.

There we go again. Another person who will thank me and tell me that they can't hire me because of my accent, as I will be dealing with people from all over the world. That it's not going to work out for their company and business, as they thought it would be difficult for these people to understand me, not only because of my accent but also because they too would have an accent and I wouldn't understand them either.

I added, probably saying too much: *"I understand I have a long way to go as far as English is concerned, especially with my accent, but I can improve by going back to school here. I didn't go to school because I don't have a permanent job and I need to pay for it and I don't want to depend on my husband for that, as I always provided for myself in Brazil since I was very young. I started working when I was thirteen years old."*

I was upset now and all I wanted was for them to leave.

Patrick looked at Romeo and asked him if he had any question or if he would like to say something and he looked at both of us and said with a smile: *"No, it's all good; I think you both covered everything there was to know."*

Patrick then told me that they were looking for a responsible person who they could trust because the person would be working alone all the time and would handle petty cash and should be pretty good in keeping records of everything.
The person should also report to them any activity and for that work they were offering a deal in the rent and a fee for getting the houses ready for move in and turnover.

Patrick then asked me, *"Do you have any questions or any doubt about this business and the company?"*

I said, *"No, I don't have any questions. Do you have any questions or something else you would like to know about me or my experience?"*

He said, "No, Romeo is right, I think we all covered pretty much everything."

And then Romeo, addressing Patrick, said, "We have to go; we have to be at the restaurant for the next meeting." Then he looked at me and said, *"Thank you, it was nice to meet you."*

I said, "Thank YOU for your time and for the opportunity to meet you both."

Without further notice Patrick then said, "We have other people that applied but we would like to try it out with you. There will be a probation time of sixty days and we would like for you to think about it and talk to your husband and give us a call or email us with your answer."

I could not believe that…they were offering me a job? Did I hear that right? Someone pinch me, please.

I looked at Steve and I said, *"That's all right, I will take the challenge."*

He said, *"No, I would like you guys to talk and to think about it and give us a call or email us later. I'm leaving this document, which is a contract, and I want you to read it because I want you to have no doubt about the job you will perform here, and if you are in agreement with what we are proposing in this document, we would like to come back and we will sign the document and we will show you around and bring you all the other documents and files from the company so you can keep them in the office or in your house if you prefer."*
"There are lots of things that we still need to go over. We need to introduce you to some contractors, gardeners, construction workers, painter and we would like to do all that then but now we have an appointment and we are running out of time."

"We don't want to go through what we've been through with previous management and we want to have that totally clear with our new manager. Think about it and give us a call or email us and we can go from there."

What else could I say by his long statement? He was being clear on his position and I just said, *"Okay, I will go over the contract and talk to Steve and will certainly get back to you. Thanks again for coming down and for your time."*

Patrick, who was already standing, shook my hand and said, "No, thank you! It was a pleasure to meet you. Steve," he said extending his hand, *"it was nice to meet you too."*

Steve replied, "Nice to meet you.

Romeo did the same and they left.

We watched them leave and I was a little airy and feeling confident and very happy for the first time in a long time. The job was mine!

Steve gave me a hug and congratulated me and we talked about the guys, their manners, and the difference between them. Steve told me he was proud of me.

We read the paper they left as a contract and we talked about it. I would not receive any money though. There would be a considerable discount in our rent and we were fine with it for the probation period. We would talk again about this later, after the probation period, but for the time being, we thought we didn't have much to lose.

It was December 1st of 2010. I emailed them back on the following morning accepting the job and they scheduled a meeting for the next morning to walk me through the business, to show me the property and to hand me the leases and other documents, etc.

When they came, they also introduced me to a family that had just moved in from Russia. The girl was supposed to sign the lease and I would be observing what I was supposed to do from that moment forward with other guests and tenants.

Between December 3rd and 15th, my official start day of work, I was working on timetables and a huge document with a bunch of worksheets for all the information from all the leases. It was a consolidation of everything for easier control. Nobody asked me to do anything. I just did that for my own use and benefit.

Each spreadsheet had a different subject, like tenant, ex-tenants, Internet, parking spots, mailbox numbers, maintenance, water heater, air conditioning, appliances, contractors and everything else I could think of that would help me manage the property.

When I finished, I sent it to them and they absolutely loved it. Or so they told me and of course I believed them. To be honest, it was quite a piece of work.

I did other changes to improve the services. I created business cards, a professional email address for me to use, letterhead for documents. The leases would be given to tenants in a folder instead of just handing them the papers.

I also created a list of inventory of all furnished houses. There was none. I used all the skills I had and applied them to my new job.

I prepared a letter introducing myself to the tenants and added it to the letter they provided me to handle to all the tenants where they were introducing us as the new managers. In the letter, among other things, they told the tenants that we were tenants as well, so our privacy would be appreciated and if they needed to talk to us, to schedule an appointment instead of knocking on our door.

From the time of the meeting until the day I officially started, I'd done way more than I was asked for. I was a professional and I was just applying what I'd learned from past experience and it felt good.

Before I started, my new bosses asked me to be patient because the previous manager was having trouble letting go of the job. The manager who was in charge when I started was actually working under the ex-manager's supervision. I'd never heard of anything like that. So now, I was guessing, I would probably have a problem and that's the reason I wrote a letter to all the tenants introducing myself. I would not take orders from another person other than my actual bosses.

I was introduced to the gardeners, a couple who also lived on the property. In fact, they lived next door to me. We shared the kitchen wall. The wife, a sweet young lady, was the manager, mostly taking orders from the previous manager who refused to let go of his position. I was also introduced to a painter and also to a contractor who was doing some remodeling in the bathroom to make it a roll-in shower for wheelchair access.

The landlords gave me total freedom to do whatever I felt it was right. They encouraged me to find things that needed to be improved.

When I officially started working and met the contractor who was working in a bathroom of one of the houses, I found out that he had the keys to all houses and storage and I told my bosses I would prefer to have control of that from that point forward, because, if I was responsible for the property I wanted to make sure I knew what was going on there. And, for a contractor to have keys to the houses when I was the manager was not an option, as I was not comfortable with that. I didn't want to be responsible for the property if someone else had the keys to the houses, furnished or unfurnished.

That was my job to do and not a contractor that would come and tell me, actually to tell the ex-manager, about it. If I was to be the manager, I didn't want anybody trying to make me look incompetent and do my job for me.

Needless to say that it created a problem, not only with the contractor, but also with the former manager, who didn't want to let go of management. I guess I had just created a couple of enemies. That was not good.

Because the contractor was upset with me when I told him I would like to have the keys, he asked the owners for a meeting and to his unpleasant surprise, I was going to be present as requested by them. Okay, now it would be a confrontation. That sounded wonderful, not to say, terrible. But I was up to the battle and so the day of the meeting arrived.

During the meeting, he would not look at me, not once, and I was trying to keep a straight face. Sorry, but it was pretty funny, not to say, pathetic. Here I was, in front of a contractor, who was at least fifteen years older than I was and he was acting like a child.

He started saying that he wanted to have things straight from the beginning so there would be no problem. I totally agreed with that.

Then he said that he never had a problem before with the managers and he wanted to have the keys to the houses and storage.

I told him that I had nothing against him, but I didn't want him to come to work whenever he wanted to, and that there should be some type of control on how many hours he was working. Besides, I needed to notify tenants that a contractor would be working on the property, especially when he had to go behind their houses.

There should be privacy and I would like to let tenants know in advance about any job performed in the property, especially if the contractors needed to work at or around their house.

The meeting ended and I was annoyed. I didn't want the atmosphere to be heavy; it was a work environment, and I had that situation before and it was not good. This type of situation never ends up on good terms.

A few days later he finished the work he and his team were performing in the house and I was never part of that anyhow since I was not working there when he started so that was one thing that he would never talk to me about anyway. I was totally fine with that.

The house was furnished by another contractor and I was asked to oversee the delivery of the furniture. It was all good. The following day I would meet the wife of one of the owners, as she was a designer and would bring all other stuff to finish the project and the house was ready to receive the new guests. It would be my first time receiving the guests and handling all the paperwork, collecting the fees and showing the property by myself.

The guests arrived around 9 pm and after all the introduction and paperwork signed, I showed the house and how things worked in the house, informed them where the garbage area and guest parking were located, etc. Then, I went back home and sent the owners an email informing them that the guests had arrived and everything was fine.

At about 11:35 pm my phone rang and it was the new guest calling and telling me that the house was flooding. That she was trying to give her son a shower and the water was going everywhere else but the drain.

I hung up and got up, as I was in bed, dressed as fast as I could and rushed to the house which was just a couple of houses down from mine.

I cleaned the mess myself, as there was no handyman or any other worker living in the property and it had to be done fast, otherwise the water would damage the wood floors in the bedroom.

When everything was dried and clean I apologized for the inconvenience and told the guests I would get back to them as soon as I could.

90

I left her house, leaving a message for the owners first and then to the contractor.

I got home and sent an email to the owners with a copy to the contractor, with all the details of what had happened, and a couple of minutes later Romeo called me very upset. He asked me what was going on and I explained to him that the bathroom was not leveled, and that the water was not going to the drain; instead it was going to the bedroom. He asked if I called the contractor and I told him I called him and left him a message to call me urgently because the bathroom was flooding and that he had not called me back yet.

Romeo apologized for all the trouble and especially for the late hours, and he thanked me for my quick action telling me he would call "the guy" — those were his words — and that he would have to fix the problem first thing in the morning.

He then replied to my email addressing the issue to the contractor and told him to have his crew back and fix the problem immediately or he didn't need to come back ever again.

I sent an email to the family who had arrived to inform them that the contractor would be in the house at 8 am and the lady replied asking for him to come later because they had arrived late and wanted to sleep in. She asked if he could come at nine instead.

After she sent me the email she called me right way to make sure I got the email and confirming her request for them to come at nine instead.

Even though we spoke on the phone I replied to the email just to have it documented and added everyone involved so everybody had the information. I have no idea what time I went to bed that day.

That day, I learned what it really meant to be a property manager.

The next morning the contractor came to my house first thing and was all nice to me, for the first time since we'd met. I went with him to the house and left him and his crew to do their thing and when I got home, I sent an email with the updated situation.

I have never seen anybody redo a job so fast in my life. By noon, everything was done, and I mean, completely done, and the problem was corrected. He used a powerful heater to dry the cement and everything. I was impressed. I tested the shower and the water was contained well and was going to the drain properly.

I sent another email with the new update and thanked "the guy," as my boss would say, and the peace returned. Or did it?

Days went by and he continued sending the emails he was supposed to send to me, to the landlords. He didn't get it that if you hire a manager it's because you don't want to bothered with minor things. Manager is a liaison between a higher level and contractors/other employees, and in my case, tenants as well, period!

I didn't say anything though. It was not worth it. After a few emails Patrick replied to one of his emails and asked him to email me with any questions, advice or quotes.

The gardeners and painter started complaining to me about the way the contractor was treating them. I witnessed when that happened a couple of times and I could not let that happen, as he didn't have any business to do with them. So I talked to him about it and he asked for another meeting with the owners. Ai, ai, ai. What are we, children? But, I didn't say anything again and he sent an email to the owners.

This time there was only Patrick, me and the contractor in the meeting. Anyway, he said he was not happy with the situation and repeated, like he did in the first meeting, that he never had any problem with anybody before and that he still thought he needed the keys to the houses without having to call me all the time he needed to come to perform a job. He said everything he wanted and it was my turn.

I told him I understood his frustration but that was something that I would prefer to continue my way, I mean, having the keys myself. I also asked him to keep it professional and I didn't want him to call me sweetie again. Besides the fact that I didn't feel comfortable when he called me that, we were in a professional environment so we should keep it that way and I added that only my husband or my close friends called me sweetie.

I also told him I didn't want him yelling or asking the other workers, who were not related to his company, bossing them around and asking them to do things. He was not their boss or supervisor and if he needed something from them to speak with me first.

He seemed shocked when I finished and he apologized and said that he was trying to be nice to me by calling sweetie and that he would respect my decision.

The meeting was over and after he left, Patrick asked me to tell them anything that was inconvenient for me. He was surprised because I didn't tell them about all the little things that were happening. I didn't want to bring these types of problems. Why would I? As long as I could handle the situation I didn't need to tell them that but he asked me to let them know if those things happened again.

Later that night I received an email, which I was in blind copy, from Romeo responding to the contractor's email. Romeo had responded to him saying that he was sorry he was asking for them to opt between him and I and if that was the way he wanted things to be, then he had no choice but honor his decision. He added that it was the first time they had such a good manager on the property and they would not let go of me just because we couldn't work together.

I was shocked when I read the contractor's email to my bosses, and I was stunned by the answer to him. I didn't want any of this to happen. It was not my choice or my conspiracy for him to be terminated. It was his suggestion and I was incredibly surprised by the owner's decision in favor of me. It felt incredibly good to see and receive the trust of two great people and I was grateful for them and for my job.

Next morning Romeo called me and they came to meet with me and I told them this was a situation that I never expected and they only repeated what they wrote in the email and asked me if I could find someone else to be a handyman. I said I could and I was going to bring three estimates from other contractors.

I called the painter they already had and asked him for a referral and he told me about his friend Miguel. I called Miguel and asked him if he could come to the office and called two other contractors I found on the web.

Miguel ended up being the guy I chose for many reasons. I presented them all the three estimates with my recommendation, which they accepted without a question.

I could not be happier with my choice. Miguel was amazing. He was a complete contractor and he did it all. Within a few days we had him on the property; he was very respectful and super reliable. As I said, I really couldn't be happier with my choice.

With Miguel as the handyman and Manuel as the painter I would focus on the day to day part of my job because they always did what I asked without me having to be on them all the time. Asked and done! I like that. I like that a lot!

A couple of years later I lost Manuel, as he left San Diego, and Miguel introduced me to another painter, who didn't do everything but he was, at the time, a good fit and it worked out good to this day.

I had a few problems in the beginning with the housekeeper. Some guests would complain about cleaning and I had to replace a few of them. Here they seem to clean the surface, not a deep clean as the housekeepers in Brazil do.

I finally found someone reliable, who cleans the way I ask and guests expect, and I'm happy with her.

Working at this place gave me the opportunity to meet so many great people from around the world and it made me realize how our life can change in a split of a second and made me also even more grateful for my life.

Talking about people from all over the world, I need to share this one and I hope people will not get mad at me for doing it. As I said, there are so many wonderful things about this country that it's easy to be lost in certain customs if we don't pay attention and, especially, if we don't speak the language.

I met a family who came from Brazil and stayed one month at the facilities I was managing and then they found a more permanent house and we stayed in contact. They always invited me to their house for parties and barbecue. Like all Brazilians, they were wonderful people. They didn't speak English very well and asked me to help them with certain things and I even taught them a bit of English.

After about two months, they moved out to that new place, I came to visit and they brought me a couple of letters the manager of their place left at their door.

I read the letter and it was about them not paying their electric bill and they told me they never received any bills before so I called SDG&E to find out what was going on. The representative informed me that they have been sending the bills and the warning letter informing they would shut off their services. So I hung up and asked to see their mail and they told me they never received any mail. That was strange because I checked the address SDG&E had and it was correct. So I asked them where their mailbox was and they looked at me with an interrogation mark on their forehead.

I explained that every condominium had their mailboxes and asked to see their set of keys they received when they moved in and there it was…a little mail key and I asked for their lease or any paperwork, as I figured the information about the mailbox number was probably there, somewhere in the folder.

Sure enough, there it was, and I took them outside to find their mail. Their mail was full of all kinds of mail, including the bills and letters from SDG&E and cable and TV bills. Mystery solved!

I spent the next couple of hours paying their bills over the phone with their credit cards and setting up for direct pay. Bless their hearts!

On another occasion, I was driving with a member of that family and she was driving us back to their house for me to get my car. We went to the drugstore to find the type of product they needed and they couldn't find anywhere. I'm telling you, it's hard to live in another country if we don't speak the language and I admire those brave people who live this way.

Anyway, she was driving and I noticed that she was not turning right with the red light and I told her she could go, if there was no red arrow on the traffic light or a sign saying "No on Red," meaning we can't turn on red as long as it was safe. She was all concerned and asked if I was sure, then she looked at me and said, "Oh my God, that's why people always get mad at me and honk on me! That's terrible!! I feel so bad now. I have been driving like this since when we arrived and it's been almost one year. I had no idea."

We both laughed and talked about the differences between our countries. How amazing America is. Brazil is so far from being this great and it's totally understandable why so many people do anything to live here.

Seven of the houses that were furnished were adapted for people who had SCI (spinal cord injury) as I said before, and these people come from all over the world for physical therapy at a facility nearby or for vacation. We were the only ones offering a facility with a roll-in shower and hospital bed and shower wheelchair for them and they were thankful for that.

When someone has such a traumatic change in life like SCI, they need to learn to do things all over again. Whether it's to eat with the other hand, or perhaps with the help of either hands, or whatever it is that they need to readapt as they lose the control of their body, it's hard to imagine how a little thing can make a huge difference in their lives.

I've learned a lot with them and I started asking for feedback because the units were to be used by them and they knew more than anybody what they needed, and I started using their feedback to improve the houses even more. Like putting handles on the cabinets, making the place for soap and shampoo in the bathroom modified for them, changing the door knobs from the round ones we had to the ones they suggested. It was amazing how we do not realized little details that we take for granted and that mean a lot to them.

This part of my job was the most incredible experience I've ever had and the most rewarding, as I felt I could make a little difference in the lives of those who would come and stay in the facilities.

It was not part of my job but I would take those who didn't rent a car or didn't have their own when coming from other states to the supermarket the day they arrived so they could at least settle down and relax a bit before hiring a taxi or deciding to rent a car. That would be my courtesy to them and it always made me feel good about it.

I was supposed to have water and flowers for them when they arrived but I started to leave some fruits and tea as well, as some of them would arrive too late at night so they could have something to eat the following morning.

I also created a sheet with information of restaurants nearby, taxi options, medical supply companies, supermarkets, shopping centers and later on I added caregivers and other services people used while living there and recommended to me in case someone asked for. Later, I started to add this document to their folder when they arrived.

I changed things a little and they appreciated me for doing that. The most rewarding thing for me though was the fact that the owners trusted me and that feeling always made me go back in my memories and remember the other leaders I had the pleasure to work with in Brazil that trusted me as much. I'm proud to say that my bosses in Brazil trusted me to the point that I had their bank account passwords, keys to their houses and safe boxes. It's an awesome feeling when these things happen and it just makes me proud of my upbringing, and of course this make me turn my heart to my mom, who, despite the fact that she didn't have proper education, taught us to be hard workers, honest and trustworthy. These were priceless lessons.

I never became friends with tenants and our relationship are mainly professional. Some of the tenants and ex-tenants I worked and work with, are a little difficult to deal with as they don't like to follow the rules and get mad at me for pointing things out, but most of them are easy going. A few of them are amazing people and makes my life as PM much easier and enjoyable.

I love working there because I have a lot of free time to do other things. Either write my blogs, go to the gym and even work in events. It's truly a blessing.

While working as Property Manager between 2010 and 2016 I also worked with events. I also did volunteer work at an animal rescue facility in Carlsbad, as a dog walker. I did that for a few months only, because as much as I loved to interact with the dogs, my heart would hurt to think that probably most of them would not make it if they were not adopted and I couldn't do much about that, so I stopped working there. It was making me sad. I wish people were more responsible about having an animal as a pet. I wish people adopted them instead of buying them. If I had money, I would adopt them all and the cats too. I would have a sanctuary for animals.

Anyway, during this period, I also tried sales. I sold makeup from a well-known brand a couple of times but like what happened when I sold those kinds of products in Brazil, it didn't work very well. I'm definitely not good at sales so my attempt to be my own boss as a salesperson failed. I knew it wouldn't work and to tell you the truth I don't know why I even tried, not only once, but twice. I don't like sales!

I also took some classes to improve my skills and that made it possible for me to help my brother with his website and of course create my own in the learning process. Part of the training was that we had to buy our own domain name and create a website and Twitter account and Facebook page for business, which I ended up creating one for the company I was working for as Property Manager and one for myself for my travel blog.

I had an interesting year in 2012. I finally decided, with the push of my parents-in-law, to apply for citizenship. So I went to USCIS's website and did a lot of research. When I was searching, I found out about community colleges. I had no idea that they existed and much less that it was so affordable to study in these colleges. I wish I had found out about that earlier!

I applied for a citizenship course at Mira Costa College. And while I was going to classes I also applied for other courses. Now I could afford this without asking money from my husband because I had a job and a small but steady salary. Yes, after my probation period they gave me a salary!

I was very excited about my new life. School, work...life was good again.

It was also in 2012 that I got involved with a non-profit organization and I became a Volunteer Secretary. It was a great experience. I invited a musician friend of mine to play at the event and it was a success. Everybody loved it, so much so that they would play in the event again in the following two years for the annual fundraiser of the foundation. For that, I thank my friend JC and Alex and his band. JC, by the way, is that friend from Cirque du Soleil I told you about earlier in this book, you know, the one Art had known before me. See, it's all about connection and network and it proves to me that everything happens for a reason. We are all connected in this world.

I met Elaine in one of the classes I attended and when I heard her speak in class, I immediately recognized her voice. I used to watch her on the morning news from time to time and I absolutely loved her. I can say that I was a fan!

Perhaps because of our age group we were always together in class, I got to know her, and I have to tell you, she was adorable, just like when I saw her on TV.

She invited me to join her and her family for an award nomination Woman of the Year that she was a nominee and I went. There I was with her family and a friend, who was also her secretary. I felt very good about it. She had invited me to join her in her special day celebration. It was so awesome. I think I made a friend.

A few months later she invited me be part of her non-profit organization, the one I mentioned earlier.

This was another opportunity that I won't forget. Although it was unpaid volunteer work, it was such a pleasure to be part of such great group of women getting together to make this world a little better for someone, for a family, for a child.

It's been a little over four years since I met Elaine and the only thing I can say about it is that it was an amazing opportunity to work with her and the members of her organization, not to mention the learning part of it. It gave me more knowledge in the non-profit field, network opportunity and more experience for my career and life. And yes, I definitely made a friend and a very good one.

CHAPTER EIGHT

Citizenship

Now let me talk about my Citizenship.

When I applied for citizenship training, I decided that I was not going to hire a lawyer to help me with the paperwork. I was going to do it myself; no need to spend extra money, so when I decided that I was ready to take the test at the immigration office I filled out the forms myself and submitted them. I submitted the paperwork only after I had studied a lot, learning about the history of the United States, the government, and everything related to the subject. Study was the word of the moment and I was happy I was now able to study.

The day I went for the interview I was a little nervous despite the fact that I had done everything and had prepared myself for the test. Again, study was the key word in command.

I went alone. I didn't want to bother my parents-in-law. I usually do my things alone and normally I don't share much of my life either. Now you must be thinking, *Sure, what is this book about then? Looks like you share a lot!*

I know, right? That's a little strange. But I'm sharing part of my story because I believe lots of the things I went through are issues a lot of people have and go through. Immigration is such an important part of the government's affairs. Immigration became a very strong part of my life.

I said I was nervous but in reality, looking back now, I'm not sure I was nervous. I think I was more curious than anything else. At the end of the interview, the lady who interviewed me said they would send me a letter with an answer. I was confident because I had all the answers right so unless there was another issue, I was fine. I was prepared.

The interview was in March and in April I received a letter with the verdict. The letter congratulated me and informed me that I had passed the test and I would later receive another letter with an invitation to participate in a ceremony soon.

I don't know exactly how I felt. It was a mixed feeling of pride, happiness, sense of accomplishment, love, gratitude. I would soon be an American citizen.

That day I would have a dinner with my parents-in-law, as we had a date every week and I shared the news with them. They were super happy for me and they wanted to know when the ceremony would be so they could go with me.

I didn't tell my husband over the phone. I waited for him to come home.

I called my mom and told her, but I think she didn't really know what exactly that meant, but she was happy for me and I was happy to share this with her. I made her proud again.

I sent an email to my siblings to share the news. I was very happy and I wished someone from my family could come for the ceremony.

When I received the invitation letter, I found out that it would take place in Downtown San Diego on June 12 of 2012.

I emailed my family to see if they would be available and could visit me in June. I didn't tell them why; I just asked if they could visit me in June. Of course everybody works and can't take days off whenever they want. I knew it would be something a little difficult, as the expenses for air tickets would be huge because it would be not only one person but the spouse and kids as well so I didn't have high hopes.

I asked my nieces too and they couldn't come either because of school and work.

When they all said they couldn't come, I felt so sad, because I wanted someone from my blood family to be with me, but I didn't tell them that I wanted them to come to go to my Citizenship Ceremony because I didn't want them to feel guilty if they couldn't come. But now I wish I had said something. It would be a very important event for me and I really wanted to celebrate with them.

Before I received the letter, my parents-in-law shared that they were going on a trip in June and when I received the letter I realized that the date the ceremony would take place coincided with the week they were going to be out of town. They had already bought the flight tickets and made the hotel reservation.

I didn't have the heart to tell them that I would miss them in the ceremony either because, again, I didn't want them to feel guilty, so I decided that I would tell them at another opportunity about the date of the ceremony.

Steve shared with me that he would have a series of meetings and events coming up in June but I told him I wished he could come if the dates of his events did not coincide with my special event.

Of course, in May when he told me they had the training dates, sure enough, they were scheduled for the week of my ceremony.

So it would be only me. I felt really sad and alone and wished I had friends here, someone who could go with me, to be there for me. I know it sounds needy but it was important, perhaps one of the best days of my life and I would be alone. I tried to remove that from my head in the days before the event. I think I was a little depressed then. It was sad and I wanted to be happy and I was happy but I couldn't help but feel all alone.

A couple of days before Pat and Nick travelled we had our dinner and they asked who was going with me and I said I was going alone. They were very disappointed that they wouldn't be able to go with me and they promised we would celebrate when they came back and we did. The four of us, Steve and I and his parents...my American family...my family.

The day of the ceremony I left the car at the train station and took the train so I didn't have to worry about parking and I love the ride by the coast anyway. There are gorgeous views from Carlsbad to San Diego. I used to see deer in the mountains on my way to school in Old Town but I haven't seen them in more than year though.

Let me talk about train stations in the U.S. The transportation system here is amazing. You can park your car for free to ride the trains. In Brazil you have to pay parking for the day and it is not cheap. Another thing is that here, in most of the train stations there is no one to sell you the tickets; it's all automated and you have to buy your tickets in the machines and I have seen so many people having problems trying to buy their tickets. I helped many of them, now that I'm an expert in buying tickets! Now, having no English skills that would certainly be a problem for you even if someone tries to help you, because if you don't know the name of the train station you have to get off, there is no way people will be able to help you.

If we had a system like this in Brazil, they would go bankrupt because probably most of the people would take advantage of the system and not pay for the tickets at all. I see some people hiding in the restrooms here when the conductor comes to check the tickets but seriously, if this was in Brazil, it would never work. That's the difference between having education and not having it.

Okay, continuing. At the place, there was a line and everybody had their families with them. I was alone and wanted to cry.

The ceremony was very nice. There were lots of people to receive their "new" birth certificate. The family would stay in the upper level where they could see us and take pictures while we would be in the auditorium. Everybody was given a number and you should sit in order, not wherever you wanted to sit. This country is very organized, that's for sure, and I love it.

There were ushers directing us to our seats. They also gave us a little flag from the US, a handbook with the National Anthem and other important American songs and holidays. It took a while for the ceremony to start. Before it started they instructed us to raise our flags at certain points.

It was a truly beautiful ceremony. President Obama was not there of course but there was a video with him talking to us and congratulating us on our new status.

We sang the National Anthem and it was a great feeling to be singing it and feeling proud of being an American!

They called us one by one and asked us to stand and everybody would clap and whistle, and at this point if you had your family with you, you would look up to them and they would take your pictures. I wish I had someone special with me to register that moment with a symbolic picture. I was not the only one alone there though and that somehow comforted my heart and at the same time, I felt sorry for them too, which I should not because I didn't know their story and I could not just judge them, thinking they were sad. That was what I was feeling; not necessarily what they were felling. Again, it was a reflex of my own feelings. We tend to project our feelings on others.

After everybody was called they read the names of all the countries that were there, starting from A to Z and whistles would be part of every country's name and the people from that country would stand up with the little US flags up in the air with cheers, like we were instructed to. There were three Brazilians there!

They didn't call Mexico when they were supposed to and at the end they asked if they missed a country and everybody started to laugh and the people from Mexico would say their country's name. When they finally asked people from Mexico to stand up, everybody burst into laughter because there were so many of them.

It really was a beautiful ceremony and at the end we went back to the tables in the back of the room and handed them our green card and they would cut them in two pieces and give us our certificate. We were now Americans! What a great feeling.

From there I went straight to get my passport, not only because they had instructed in the package they sent us with the invitation letter but also because that would be the only way I could travel abroad and come back home.

Home. The first time I said "come back home" after I became a citizen of this great country, was when I realized that home means home and it was a great feeling calling this country home! Until then, whenever I said home while here, I didn't feel the same way as I feel when I say it now.

Anyway, they also talked about the passport in the ceremony, as we would need a passport now that we didn't have our green card anymore.

In September of 2012 I received a letter from Mira Costa College inviting me for a ceremony that they would host for the new American Citizen that took their Citizenship classes. It was going to take place in February of 2013.

With that in mind, I decided that I wanted to go and this time I would like to have at least one member of my family from Brazil with me. It would be a simple ceremony but I wanted that because I was not able to have anybody in June.

I called my family and asked if they could visit and, again, everybody had to work and couldn't come. My niece and goddaughter, then eighteen years old, would be on school break so I talked to my sister and brother-in-law and we started planning her visit.

I made an invitation letter for her to take to the consulate, informing them that I would pay her expenses while she was visiting for a couple of weeks.

Everybody was excited and I was more excited than anybody. For the first time since I moved here I would have a member of my family visiting me. I helped them pay for her passport and of course, as promised, I was going to help with the airfare.

My niece was super excited because she would have the opportunity of her life to come visit me and go to Disneyland and all the other attractions that we have here.

She went for the interview and her visa was denied. I was so upset. Why would they do that? Okay, she didn't have a job and she didn't have a bank account. She didn't have anything, except her parents and her sister, so I guess they figured she would overstay her visa if granted.

I was so upset that I wrote a letter to the President. Let me say that again in a different way. I was so upset that I wrote a letter to the President of the United States of America, Barack Obama.

Yes, I'm that crazy…I couldn't believe they denied her visa. I'm the one person that had all the problems coming here and trying to find a job. I'm one person that would advise everyone with wrong ideas about moving to another country illegally to stay in their country because it's not easy.

The only thing I could think of was that I would never want a loved one to go through what I've been through. And I would certainly not hide someone in my house taking the risk of getting my just-acquired rights as a new citizen to be taken away from me. I had an invitation letter with all the information about my status and my willingness to help her financially. I even gave her copy of my passport, of my new status and yet her visa was denied.

So, I did what I thought it would be right to do. To bother the President of the United States of America with a problem that was not his. Get that? I guess everybody blames him for everything. Poor man…and I'm sorry and ashamed of what I did. Of course I was not blaming him. That never passed through my mind. That is one of the nicest human beings out there and he has all my respect. I was just frustrated and of course I didn't expect an answer. If that, by any chance happened, it should be a very rude one, and I deserved that.

That's who I am…I do things first then I think about it, so whatever. I got my frustrations out in the letter.

To my surprise and disbelief, a letter came to me from the White House from no less than Mr. Obama! I looked at the mail and the letter and I couldn't believe it.

He was probably inviting me to go to the White House to take back my passport. He should do that and put me in front of the entire world to teach me a lesson and I would be escorted out of the White House handcuffed and with the FBI on my heels.

Now, that would be a theme for a movie! Of course, there it is…my imagination working again.

He was apologizing for the inconvenience and shared with me his plans to work to fix the immigration system. HE was apologizing to ME.

I felt so ashamed I wrote a letter to him. Why did I do that? I'm such an idiot. The poor man has things more important to do than to deal with a whining lady about her problems with her niece's visa being denied.

I just want to apologize to President Obama now, so here it is, Mr. President, a real apology to you and thank you for being such a great President!

As I said before, 2012 was a very interesting year. Lots of things happened. I went back to school. I met a lot of interesting people. And as I became a US citizen, I had not only the right but the responsibility to vote and I did that with pleasure and a certain feeling of power.

I do not like to discuss politics or religion or even sometimes sports. Don't get me wrong; I have my own opinion and views about these subjects, and I have my choices. I just think it's pointless to argue about it, unless I'm in a position that I have to fight for rights or for a cause.

Talking about fighting for rights, I have to say this. I don't need to repeat that this is a great country, everybody knows that, but people here seem to take things for granted.
People complain about everything that they think is not right in the country but they don't do their part. They don't exercise their right to vote!

You have the power to make changes you want but you have to be involved. At least go out and vote

In Brazil it's mandatory that we vote and if we don't we have to pay a little fine and can lose certain rights and I think this is only fair.

We have the voting day on a Sunday. Every public school in town opens to receive the votes. Yes, most of people are off work and even if we are not, we have to find a way to go out and vote or justify our absence because otherwise we lose many important rights.

There, if we don't vote, we can't apply for jobs related to public services. We can't obtain a passport or ID card. We can't renew our subscription in public schools, we can't get a loan from certain institutions, and if we don't vote or justify why we didn't vote for three times our "titulo de eleitor," which is the ID card we use to vote, is cancelled and then we lose all those right forever.

As you can see, we have a lot to lose but here nothing happens if you don't vote and then when I see people complaining and protesting I wonder if they voiced their rights in the election. Here you can vote by mail so there is no excuse. There, I said it. I had to.

And I hate to say that, but it's a shame that the government in Brazil is so corrupt and doesn't take care of the people and the problems that need attention.

You have a great country here, guys, so go do your part to make it even better. Vote, people.

Anyway, while I continue seeking opportunities to grow professionally and personally, I'm enjoying the life I have.

I visit my family and friends in Brazil every year and I continue to write my blogs...oh, yes, I told you that I write blogs about travel. I talk about places to visit in Brazil. I give some tips and advice and I have fun doing that.

I always loved to travel and it's good to share the experience. Want to visit Brazil in a safe way and go to the best places there? Then look for my blog posts, subscribe, ask me questions and enjoy the ride!

CHAPTER NINE

And I Became an Actress!

Now let me share something very interesting that happened to me. At the end of November of 2013, I received an email from the organization where I volunteer in Encinitas and they asked if we were available to participate in a three days of shooting for an educational video San Diego County was creating for their website at the end of January 2014.

The video was about shelter. It was for them to show what happens when a disaster strikes in the city when all kinds of people end up in shelters. It was for training purpose. The video was going to be seen by the volunteers who work in the shelters.

I replied to the email saying that I was available but didn't really think of anything other than that I would be there to help as a volunteer, perhaps to demonstrate how to do a CPR or something like that.

They replied back saying that they would give us more information when they received it.

At the end of December, I received the email with days, time, and location and when the first day arrived, there I went.

When I got to the location, there were many people inside and I didn't notice they were filming and I went straight to the table where there were two people behind it giving information. These two people were actors and I had no idea. I asked for the person I had the information to contact once I was there and they pointed me to a lady who was seated at another table across the room. So I crossed the room and introduced myself to her and she asked me to sign a couple of documents, one which was a list of participants and the other a talent release. She then asked me to wait with the other people that were in a table next to hers. Only when I sat down that I realized that the shooting was already in progress. Well, not really; they were blocking. At that moment when I introduced myself to the other people on the table and I spoke with them I found out that they were all actors!

It was three working days and a fantastic experience. The director and his wife and crew were very nice and it was a pleasure to work with them. Three days on set and I was feeling like a star! It was great and I loved it!

This made me realize how much I love acting and since I did theater in Brazil I was surprised I didn't think of looking into it before. It really, never dawned on me that I could try that here, I mean, acting. Now that I'm thinking about it, it seemed to be a far, far away dream. I mean, every child has a dream and I always thought about myself being on TV in my dreams. I used to dance in front of the TV for my mom every time we were watching a TV show where there were dancers. So I would imitate their moves and my mom would say that I should pursue TV because I was amazing. Well, that's a mother's opinion and that's what mothers do. They look at their creations as the best ones, the most beautiful, the most intelligent, the most everything.

I always thought my mom had the highest thoughts about me and she really did. She would say all the time how beautiful I was. How intelligent I was...and I believed her...I would reply back that I was that way because she made me that way! Therefore she was beautiful and intelligent herself and she would laugh and get a kick out of it.

Anyway, after that great first experience of the three day shooting and meeting all kinds of actors on set I was very excited and found out then that most of the actors came through an agent and in the last day of the shooting Dennis, one of the actors, gave me his agent's business card.

I didn't waste time. The next morning I sent her an email telling her that I met a lot of her actors on set and asked her if she would be willing to work with me. She replied asking me to send her my headshot and resume if I had one and if she was interested in representing me she would contact me back for an interview. I emailed her back and said I would send her my headshot and resume as soon as I could.

Okay, headshot and resume. Well, I didn't have that but I went online and saw some models of resumes and voila! I created mine with the theater experience and modeling training I had in Brazil plus my experience on set here and got my headshot. Made a package and sent it to her a couple of weeks later.

She called me right way and set up an interview. In the interview, she told me it would probably be difficult to find me speaking roles in commercials because of my accent.

Big news, huh? My accent is something that has prevented me from finding regular jobs, let alone TV jobs!

To my surprise she took me, and just like that I had an agent! I was speechless. How can I not consider myself a lucky girl?

But see, with that one opportunity I was able to find an agent who believed in me. Who saw something in me, and that made me believe in myself.

From that experience, other opportunities came to me for TV commercials and I'm embracing and enjoying every part of this new chapter of my life. Another opportunity to learn and as I always loved films, TV and theater, this just gave me more desire to keep learning about the art of acting.

This event also gave me the opportunity to meet some really nice people and professionals, some of whom I'm still friends with.

From that opportunity many other doors opened for me and I can also tell you that from that one volunteering opportunity so far I was able to participate in at least sixteen indie films as an actress, plus a bunch of commercials and many other industrial projects and photoshoots.

111

Furthermore, I also received an invitation to help on set and be paid as a PA (Production Assistant). I was invited, and became a producer of a talk show. Another production company contacted me to be a publicist of one of their films and, I have to tell you, I did pretty good and scored a couple of TV, radio and podcast interviews.

I had a lot of funny moments going to auditions. I usually don't go to audition for commercials that have speaking roles because I know I probably won't be chosen. And no, you may think that I'm a very negative person or that I should believe in me. Yes, I do believe in me and I'm capable of doing anything; however, I know my limitations and I know I will not book a speaking role in a commercial because of my accent, period. Unless it is a very specific part that they need a native from Brazil to speak Portuguese or have a Portuguese accent, and that is not common. Otherwise, I would be wasting not only my time and money, but their time as well. If I can send a taped audition, great; otherwise, if I apply I just say that I have an accent and send them a link to my reel.

Interesting enough, as I finished writing this book, I happened to book not one, but two speaking roles in two industrials. So maybe things will change one day and that taboo will be broken.

For now, I'm happy with all the opportunities I have and all thanks to the wonderful job I have, which gives me time to pursue this acting career.

Now, do you remember I told you about a little problem I had and I would tell you about? Well, the time to give you that information is now.

You know, wherever you work, sometimes you don't get along with everybody and in the acting word, it's not different and it happens too.

I was cast to work as an actor on a really cool project that had to do with work environment. The project consisted of how different we are and how to deal with every type of person, who has a different opinion on things that can cause problems at work as we are all different, and how we all have our own personalities.

At some point in the training process, we had to not exactly confront the other person on why they would have a different take on things than us, but we had to talk about our own take about a subject and explain why we

112

had that opinion. And, there was this guy that was completely on the opposite side, from what my opinion was.

While all the other people were moderately evenly distributed, this person and I were the extremists.

Each of us was on the extreme side of this wall and for me he seemed to be very arrogant. In his mind, he was just ambitious but it came across, not only for me, but also for everybody. He was pure arrogant.

I mentioned this because it really is about opinion. Everybody is different and has all the right to be and think whatever way they do but when you are in a work environment, you have to hear the other person, even if it's hard. Sometimes, the way we say things we are misinterpreted and misunderstood. I absolutely loved that project and in particular learned a lot about myself and it made me realize that we really need to be willing to listen, but we also can't let the other person dominate the situation imposing only his or her way. Our strength and weakness can work perfectly together. This video training was an eye opener and I totally recommend the program to everybody.

It was a little uncomfortable, I believe, not only for me, but for the entire group, because I would tell what I thought of him to his face and that, for some people, is very rude. But it's not in my world. I know I probably should have more tact but this person was just too much and it became clear to everybody that the two of us were having our little war going on between us.

A couple of months later, I was invited to be a part of the same project again, due to my position and I loved it. Thankfully, he was not invited. I have worked with him a couple of other times after that and it was not bad, although we were not working side by side on these other projects. But just recently I had an audition and guess who was there to be my partner at the audition? Yep! There you go. This acting world is very small and truth to be told, I looked at him in a totally, different way. He is actually a nice person, or perhaps he changed, or I did.
Anyway, I've come to a realization that life is a huge school and that you have to keep moving forward and upward, and for that, there is no other way but keep learning, whatever you feel like. Nothing you learn will be

wasted and everything adds up and you feel your spirit enlightening with every lesson.

I never thought I would meet so many professionals in the entertainment industry and stay connected with them and participate in their projects and here I am, writing about it.

I'm doing this because I want people to know we can do everything we want in this life. Sometimes opportunity knocks and it's up to us to first, recognize it, then accept it and embrace it and go from there and expand.

Fear? Fear of what? To make a fool of yourself in front of others? To fail? I'll tell you how you will fail. You fail if you don't try!

Of course none of this would've happened if I didn't do my part. Yes, I went to take classes, acting classes. And because I have an agent that doesn't mean that I just sit at home and wait for her to do all the work. She has many actors to represent and there is a limit on how many actors she can send to an audition so of course she is not going to send all the actors to every opportunity all the time. And she is not going to send actors who don't fit the role. So yes, I have to go after jobs too. I have to do my part. I have to find jobs and submit myself too.

So, dream big and go after your dreams, whatever they might be. Work hard and know that you are worth with all your uniqueness. Yes, you are a unique human being and whatever way you are, you are loved and appreciated and you are perfect just the way you are.

I really didn't come here for the American Dream. I didn't want to go back to school but it was because I was frustrated and because I would have to depend on my husband to pay for my studies and I didn't want that to happen. Plus, I didn't know about the community colleges. That was a great find and I wanted to share this with everyone who may read this book. If you don't have the means to go to a regular college, believe me, a community college will do wonders for you.

I take classes from time to time now. In fact, this year I enrolled in Spanish classes. I do speak Spanish but I want to improve my ability to speak the language and I'm sure I will have more work opportunities in this fairly new career which I absolutely love, if I speak Spanish.

I discovered a completely new world with acting, and I'm so happy doing it. I take every opportunity I have to be on set to help to tell a story. I just participated in a workshop about writing a screenplay. I'm so in love with everything that has to do with art now. Actually, I always loved any form of art. I used to oil paint in Brazil…that's art too and I love it. I would love to paint again and I will take classes here one of these days.

I hope this will give you some inspiration. I didn't write this book to be famous. I wrote it because I wanted to share this part of my life with you so you can be more prepared if you one day decide to do the same thing. If you decide to immigrate to another county, do yourself a favor and reinvent yourself. You will certainly need that.

Also, if an opportunity knocks on your door, grab it with both hands and don't let go because opportunities usually don't knock twice, so pay attention to what is happening in your life. The Universe sends signs all the time; we just have to open our eyes to see it, and our hearts to feel it and connect with whatever the Universe is trying to show us.

I met a couple of good friends in San Diego and even Los Angeles. In the acting world, this is not so easy. But there is this small group of people that is very special to me and I hope it will stay this way for a long time.

CHAPTER TEN

Visiting Brazil and making comparisons

Every time I visit my family in my home country, I can't stop comparing the two countries.

Yes, I love my home country but it has a lot to grow and to improve. The difference is huge in every sense. Roads, streets, transportation system, even the trash pickup is different here.

They need to invest more in education and keep kids at school longer so they don't get involved in violence and crimes. They need to pay decent salary to teachers. They need to pay decent salaries for those who put their lives at risk to protect the population. They need to invest in the public hospitals. They need to get rid of bad politicians who get the job just to become rich with public money. There are so many things they need to do that it's hard to imagine how and when that will happen.

It's sad that I have to admit that my home country is far from perfect and I don't believe there is a country or anything that is perfect but one could dream to have a decent life in a place they can call home. Their home country should give them this feeling. Instead, it doesn't happen, and, millions of people leave their countries each year to try to make a better life for themselves and their families, and some of them end up worse than they were.

I never thought of moving from my country to another country to have a better life and I didn't move to the United States to have that. My story is different. As I said, I met a very decent man from this country, and we got married and that's why I ended up here.

I know many people here who work seven days a week just to pay their bills. They can't even go visit their families in their home country. Maybe they are happy that way, but I ask, *is that really different from what they had in their home country?* I don't know; I can't tell because I'm not in their shoes.

I know one thing for a fact, and I can give this as advice, and I will say that again. If you move to another country, prepare yourself for it. Go back to school and study as hard as you can. Change your field of work if necessary. You will probably have to do that. Be persistent and never give up. The so-called American Dream still exists but you have to do your part to deserve it and to enjoy it and to live it! Better yourself, study, work hard, respect the rules here and the people here, take every opportunity to learn. That way you will be closer to realizing your dream.

I said that once and I will say it again: if you come here illegally and believe you will be successful, believe me, that is not going to happen, or at least it is going to be very difficult, especially if you have little or no education.

You probably don't know this if you are reading this book in another country. In fact I believe you have no idea, but there are hundreds of homeless people on the streets here, including American citizens! Yes, you read that right: American citizens! And I'm not talking about the people who came here and became American citizens, like I did. I'm talking about people who were born here and lived here their entire life. That show you it's not easy. The perception we have of America when we don't live here is different from the reality.

No, I never had the American Dream and yet, here I am, living it and I have to say that I love it!

I came here legal and I'm now a citizen of this country, and I'm very proud of it. For me it was an unforgettable experience with a lot of learning experience and I'm grateful for every opportunity I had and continue to have here. And I would tell anyone who would ask, that if they believe they will find a job right way in the field they have their diploma from college, unless they are qualified with very special skills needed here, it will be much harder than they think.

This is my story and, as I said, it's not my intention to make it to be a guide for anyone. This is not a how-to type of book. I just talk about my own experience.

I know people who came here and tried to succeed and as it didn't work, they went back to their country. I'm sure it was also a great experience for them and they loved it here or maybe not. What do I know? I don't know the reasons they went back to their country and I can think of some reasons which I'm not going to talk about because it would be only speculation on my part. I like facts and I could never know for sure, so why even write that down?

If you are from another country and are reading this book and thinking about embarking on your adventure, moving to another country, whatever country you may be thinking about moving to, I would never tell you not to do that. But if you decide to take the chance, then I would say this: *go back to school and study hard, better yourself, work hard and network.* Those will probably be your best bets, but there will be no guarantee so think it through before you make your decision. Decision made, good lucky on your journey.

The United States is a great and a beautiful country and to be able to live here is a dream for many foreigners like me, but again, the so-called American Dream, whatever that may mean to you, is not for everybody. Or, at least, it's way harder to get than you think. Yes, it's possible, but don't you dare think for a second it's easy. I keep repeating it because it is important to point these things out, as it's not going to be easy.

Don't compare yourself with others. Don't compare your life with other people's life. Don't envy anybody's life. You really don't know what they are going through. Everybody is in a different level in life. Everybody has their own struggles and you don't know anything about it unless they tell you, which they probably won't.

118

Focus on your own life and, if you can, help someone from time to time. It doesn't need to be much. Volunteer, because that can lead you to a great opportunity. When you give with heart, you will certainly receive.

If you asked me if I think I succeeded here, I will tell you this:

I had a much better job and salary in my home country when I arrived here. I have, with no doubt, a better life here and here is why: it's because I can count on my husband if I need to. Although I have a decent salary here today, it would not be enough if I wanted to have the same lifestyle I had in my home country, if I was on my own.

I used to go to the salon every week or every other week for a manicure and pedicure and I don't do this here. Well, I don't do that because truly, I never found someone that can do a great job, like manicurists do in Brazil! Well, not true, I did find someone and he is the best one here, for me…but it's very expensive and besides the regular pay, they expect you to pay for services, 15% or20%. So, I do it myself and every now and then I go to the salon. Not that I can't afford it, but because I can do it myself and I don't want to spend that kind of money all the time. The money I make has a value and I work hard for it so I won't give it away like that. Besides, if I don't go to my manicurist, I regret going because it's never good. I'm not picky but, really, the difference is huge. Loc is great and his mom does a good job too and so do the girls who work with them.

I used to go to restaurants and bars with my friends every week for happy hour after work and I don't do this here much, not only because I don't have friends here, but because it would be too expensive and my salary alone wouldn't do it, especially if I had to pay for rent and if I lived alone. If I can do that, it's certainly because I have a partner in life.

I used to travel a lot on weekends, and I don't do this here and, unless I have the help of my husband, it would not be possible for me to be doing that either with my salary. And the list goes on and on. I could say other things, like buying clothes, which I was never a shopper anyway, but if I wanted to do that I would have to earn more, and now I ask you: "How would I pay for all of that?" And I'm not even talking about health insurance, supermarket, dentist, education, medication, which are very important things! Then, there are bills such as water, electricity, phone, car insurance, gas and the list goes on.

THE AMERICAN DREAM AND EVERYTHING IN BETWEEN

If I came here chasing the American Dream and was doing that alone, I would probably be living with a roommate, working various jobs, six to seven days a week, just to maintain myself and pay my bills. And I understand that's how most people live here or wherever they live. Life is not easy for anybody. We have to keep working to survive.

Working as a Property Manager and seeing all kinds of applications and having to do the screening of many people I can tell you that there are a lot of people here living beyond their means by what I see in their credit reports or the difficulty some of them have to pay their rent on time. It's hard.

Before I forget this, unfortunately, you may hear things like this sometimes: *"Why don't you go back to your country? Don't even know how to take an order?"* Yes, I've heard that many times, in restaurants, when a server brought something different than the customer ordered. I'm not sure if the person understood what they were saying, as the servers were usually Mexicans, but I was shocked that people are so cruel and inconsiderate.

It's sad but it is a reality. There is some discrimination, but I would suggest you not to take that personally. Sometimes, people had a bad day and say things like that. They should not, but they do and there is nothing you can do about it, because if you reply in a bad manner, you will probably be fired.

As you can see, it's not easy and, again, I'm not trying to be negative and I'm certainly not complaining. How could I? I feel blessed to have a good life here and that, again, is thanks to the support of my husband and for the opportunities to work I got so far.

Truly, it's up to me to keep working and improving my skills and moving forward with my life. For that, as I said, there is only one way: education, and that, in my case, thanks to the community colleges!

I'm very happy with my life, with my job and my acting career and I have no idea what the future holds for me. I'm just grateful for what I have and I hope I can live a meaningful life. As for the future, I can't control it so I don't worry about it either.

What I learned from this experience is that life happens the way it is supposed to happen. Well, I already knew that but it just made me realize that we can't worry about future or the past. We do have to do our part, open our minds, and see the possibilities and be grateful for what we have and life will happen naturally.

They say that you write for yourself and writing this book and rewriting it countless times during the editing process made me realize that this saying is perfectly and true.

CHAPTER ELEVEN

Closing

Now, do you remember my fear of something happening to my family, especially to my mother, and I wouldn't have time or a chance to get to them?

My dearest mother had a light heart attack on April 30 of 2014. It was almost 6 pm when I received a call from my sister-in-law, and she told me my mother had had a light heart attack and was doing some tests. She said that she was fine and I went crazy here.

I checked for flights for that same day but I would not have time to get to LAX. She guaranteed me my mother was okay and I asked the name of the hospital where my mother was. I asked and she gave me the phone number of the hospital. She told me I could not talk to her as she was in an intensive care facility, for monitoring.

I called the hospital anyway and talked to the nurse, and she wouldn't give me information about my mother and I went even crazier. I begged her to tell me how my mother was because I was living in the United States and I needed to know her conditions.

She broke the rules and told me my mother was fine. She said my mother was aware of everything, she was talkative and happy, and that she was there just because they needed to have more tests done to her to make sure everything was okay. She said I should not worry about her. I asked her to tell my mother that I called her and sent her a kiss and to tell her I loved her.

That night I didn't sleep well and the following morning I called again and spoke with another nurse. The same thing happened. She couldn't have given me any information, I explained again my situation, and she told me she was with my mother at that very moment. She was taking a bath and then would eat. I asked her to tell my mom that I called and she yelled from where she was that Isabel was on the phone. I heard my mom saying something and the nurse laughed and told me that my mom was all happy and proud, saying that I was her daughter who lived in the States.

We both laughed and I asked her to give my mom a hug and a kiss and tell her I was thinking of her and loved her. The nurse told me that my mother was doing fine, for me not to worry and that she was there just to do some tests and I was then more relaxed, and when I hung up I started looking for flights and making plans to visit my family on Mother's Day, which would be the following weekend.

I went to work, as I had a commercial to shoot, and when I got home that day, after I took a shower and was relaxing and reading in bed, I received a call from my sister-in-law. It was around 9 pm…it was 1 am in São Paulo. She didn't need to say anything…I just started crying and she told me that my mother had another heart attack and didn't resist, that they did everything to try to revive her but had no success. Just like that, she was gone. That very fear happened on May 1 of 2014.

In Brazil when we die we are buried the same day if we die early in the morning, or if we die in the afternoon, we are buried in the next morning. Even if I had a flight, I wouldn't have time to arrive there on time for her funeral. The only thing that eases my heart is that she didn't suffer and she was not sick, trapped in a hospital bed for days or months, suffering with a terrible illness.

Now, the question someone would ask me if I think I succeeded here I would ask back after this book. Do you think I did? What does success mean to you?

THE AMERICAN DREAM AND EVERYTHING IN BETWEEN

All I can say is that I'm blessed to be able to have the job I have and to have all the opportunities that I have to work doing what I love, which is acting. Being an actor here is for sure a dream come true and it's without a doubt the only reason that I kept going after my mom passed way.

If I didn't have that passion in my life, I would be very depressed. Unfortunately, my mom never saw any of my work as an actor here but I told her all about what was going on two months prior to her death in a phone conversation. I used to call her every other week and in the last couple of years, I started to call her every week.

She was thrilled for me. I could see her eyes shining as if I was in front of her. She was the proudest mother on earth and this is what kept me going.

Every little acting gig I get, it's of my mom that I think. I wish she were here for me to call her and tell her all about it.

It's been over two years since my mom passed away and it's still painful for me to call home because I know she is not going to answer the phone and tell me she knew it was me...or that she was just thinking of me...that she knew I was going to call her that day. Oh, how I miss her.

I've been blessed my entire life and all the lessons I learned from my mother when I was a child I'll never forget, and I'm so grateful for my mother and my family.

I had a very limited life when I was a kid, in terms of money. I was very poor and my family and I came a long way, and the last ten to fifteen years of my mom's life were, without a doubt, the best years of her life and I'm very happy that she was able to see her kids succeed in their lives. I'm very happy she realized some of her dreams. One of her dreams was to own a home and we were able to buy one, the same home that I go to and stay in when I visit my family. We bought the house when I was 25 years old.

It was a very ordinary house but it was ours, and we, the family, worked together and improved it a lot and we were able to give our mom a decent and well-deserved home and life. All of the sacrifices she made when we were kids, we were able to return to her, at least a little bit. So I hope.

Now, as I finish writing this book, my oldest nephew died in a car accident in Brazil on September 11, 2016 and I was not able to go for his funeral. All I could do was to call my sister to offer my support. I just hope that my family feels my love for them.

As you can see, being an immigrant is not all flowers.

Life is precious. Family is a treasure. Friends are valuable pearls and we need to keep them all close to our hearts.

This is a picture of my mom and I. We took it on a New Year's Eve. I miss her…*minha cabiçudinha bunitinha*!

This is about Ana, my mother!

The more I think about my mother the more I realize how beautiful and precious she was.

I never saw my mother cursing anyone or her situation.

I always saw her sitting quietly and very thoughtfully.

I never saw my mother going to someone else's house and talking about other people's lives. In fact, I never saw her talking about other people's lives at all, for that matter.

I constantly saw her praying silently. She always had a serene and tranquil face. Her faith in God was everything and I believe He honored her and blessed her and I thank Him for that.

If someone mistreated her, she got hurt but she never shot back in the same way. She would ask why they were doing that. Why they were treating her like that.

She never engaged in fight or argument. She would leave and cry alone... And pray.

She always treated others with respect, even when she didn't agree with them. She always said, *"God sees everything."*

She was for sure a very enlightened spirit with a beautiful soul.

She taught her kids to respect others, especially the elders. She taught us to stand up when an older person or a person physically injured or pregnant woman approached us, so they could sit. Even though she never had the opportunity to go to school, she knew what was right.

She was a strong woman, a woman who was always there for me and loved me more than anyone else in the entire world could ever love me.

She was generous and forgiving.

She worked hard all her life until we, her kids, were able to provide for her and get her out of work. She didn't want to stop working but accepted staying home, so much we insisted her to stay home and stop working for others. She never really stopped working and she would lovingly cook and care for the house.

My mother loved me so much. She spoiled me so much. Not that type of spoiling that the child turn into a spoiled brat. No. She knew my favorite food and my favorite desert and made it often. On weekends, she would bring my breakfast in bed!

On weekends when I was watching TV on the living room, many times, I fell asleep and I woke up with my blanket over me. Even when I didn't fall sleep and was just curled up in the couch, she went to my bedroom and get my blanket for me.

She brought me tea and popcorn all the time. She even made me corn meal and all this as an adult.

127

This happened so many times and I don't know what I've ever done to deserve such love and devotion.

She did that not only with breakfast. She would make what we call "bolinho de chuva", here they have that at Denny's (pancake puppy), and if I was not home, she would save a bunch for me. If I were home studying or reading in my bedroom she would bring them to me with tea. Her tea was the most delicious tea I have ever tasted. It may be silly, but it's true. I can make them anytime and I can try anyone else's but none will be like my mother's. The ingredient must be love.

She knew which part of the chicken I liked the most and would not let anyone eat that. It was mine! My sister always got upset because she too, liked it, gizzard! Sometimes I would share with her and my mother too.

When she made belly pork, she made mine first and separate them. She made them for me the way I liked it, not all the way crunchy. In fact, they were not crunchy at all and that's the way I liked it. I was not always a vegetarian, unfortunately.

Many times, I caught my mom looking at me with such intense look. I firmly believe she was praying for me. I can't say that for sure and when I asked what was that about, she replied saying: *"Nothing."*

Same way, many times while my mom fell asleep on the couch when we were watching TV together, at night or on the weekends, I would look at her and so many things came to my mind. All the things she went through when I was child and then, as adult. I always, on my way, ask God to protect and bless her.

I never met anyone who met my mother who didn't love her. She was the light of our family.

Onde quer que a senhora esteja mãe, saiba que eu te amo e sinto muito a sua falta! Wherever you are mom, know I love you and miss you dearly!

FUNNY STORIES

This part of the book is just some funny things that happened to me while living here. This will sound like a standup comedy. Hope you will see that way and enjoy it and please, do not take any of these seriously.

Being an immigrant in this country has been quite an adventure for me. First of all, every time someone asks me where I'm from and I respond I'm from Brazil they go:

- *Hola, como estas? Bien venida.*

If I tell them, it's hard for me to find acting job because of my accent the first thing they always say is:

- *But look at Sofia Vergara!*

I always feel the need to explain that she is Spanish speaker. That there are thousands of Spanish speakers on TV, commercials or TV shows, but we don't see Brazilians a lot. And when I say this they say,

- *"But you speak Spanish too!"*
- *That doesn't matter, the problem is the accent. They go by the accent. Mine is from Portuguese.* That's my answer and they go like: *"Oh."*

It never fails. People, please… we speak Portuguese in Brazil, not Spanish… Yes, I understand the language and speak it too but my primary language is Portuguese. I give them some credit though; after all, Brazil is the only country in South America where the people speak Portuguese instead of Spanish.

Sometimes when they hear I'm from Brazil the go like:

- *"Oh, cool, I've been to Buenos Aires…* or *Argentina."* It's like me responding to them when I learn they are from the States… *"Oh, I've been to Canada* or *Mexico"* or another state in another country.

A couple of people asked me if the Capital of Brazil is Buenos Aires or Rio de Janeiro.

It's funny! Anyway… That's that.

∞

Looking for a job was a saga for me. After I got married, I used to spend all day and most of the evening applying for jobs on the companies' websites and sending my resume through Craigslist. That was definitely not fun!

It took me more than three years to find a decent job…and I love my job now… the only time I don't like is when I receive a call or email from the tenants…

They only call me or email when they have a problem… They don't call me or email me to ask me how I'm doing…or to join them for dinner… or wine and cheese… No, it's always to fix a problem they created.

I'm telling you, tenants are a lot of trouble… they create all kinds of problems!

Some of them are very rude. Some don't like to follow the rules and always yell at me and get all defensive whenever I need to point out an issues.

Although I have to say, some of them are the most amazing people I've ever met and make my life as a Property Manager much better and they are the reason I'm happy doing this job. That's for sure! And I'm sure they know who they are to, in case they read this.

∞

My parents-in-law are a blessing and my best friends here. We have a date every week and there are so many laughs.

They always tell me, especially my father-in-law, that I should speak slower, to slow down so people can understand me better. In fact, my father-in-law advised me that I should speak slower because American people are slow. His words, not mine! I sincerely never thought that way but lately I have been thinking a lot about how President Obama speaks when he addresses the Nation and I'm starting to believe he thinks the same way!

I love the way Obama speaks. I will try to make an appointment with him and ask him where he got trained to speak so perfectly... you know, as per a certain politician he is not American. The system must be broken... I thought only citizens born in the country could be President. I'm so naïve! I know nothing about anything.

∞

Most of the interviews I had the honor to be invited to participate in ended up with something like this:

You have a great resume and I'm sure you are great at what you do, but we can't hire you due to your accent. Eighty percent of your job would consist of spending time on the phone and I'm afraid my clients won't understand you.

It was so frustrating. That was energy draining, really...

After so many tries with no success, I start searching for Administrative Assistant jobs and got a few offers for one or twice a week, two or three hours a day in a home office type of business separating and filling documents... That's it!

I kept trying...next level...Receptionist... I just wanted to have my foot in the door then I could prove I was capable, because I really was... No luck...they wanted Spanish-speaking and in the end, I would lose for a native Spanish speaker. If not that, they would prefer an American who had the ability to speak the language... Great!

Keep moving down… Waitress…no…had no experience…long after I stopped applying for waitress position I met a Brazilian who worked in a restaurant near my house and I asked her how she got the job. Well, turns out she lied and said she told them that she used to work at McDonalds! She told me that's how people get their jobs as waitress: just lie and hope that nobody is going to call your country to find out.

What? I was so naive! But at this point I really didn't want to be a waitress anymore, so the hell with it. I'm not going to lie. I could feel my face blushing just thinking about lying in the interview! What a fiasco! Besides, I was afraid I would not be able to know the menu by heart! That's ridiculous, isn't it?

After two long years working part-time and in sporadic minor jobs, the job came to me, just like that.

One day I saw two guys coming down the street where I lived and I closed the blinds. They were going door to door and I thought they were those religious people who want to convert you to their religion. Thanks, people, and I respect your religion but I have my own beliefs and I don't want anybody trying to force me to hear what they have to say or try to convince me to go to their church. I know it's honorable what you do, trying to recruit more sheep for your God, but I can talk to God myself. We are buddies and I have a direct line with Him in my house!

Anyway, religion is something I don't talk about. I believe in whatever I want to believe. I believe in God, I believe in angels, I believe in spirits, good and bad, I believe in energy, good and bad, and I totally respect other people's beliefs as well. If they don't believe in anything, it's all right. So we are all good.

∞

One day, probably after two or three months that I had been working as a Property Manager, one of my bosses came to visit me. Not really to see me, but to see their property and see how things were and we started to walk the complex, and I was showing him things that needed to be done, etc. and he asked me after I finished if there was anything else and so this is how the conversation went from that point of our meeting.

Boss: *So, is there anything else going on that we need to take care of?*

Me: *Well, just the new tenant that just moved in. She needs new bulbs.*

Boss: *What?*

Me: *The new tenant needs new bulbs.*
Boss: *She needs what?*

Me: *She needs bulbs for the living room. There are a few burnt.*

Boss: (he started laughing and was almost rolling on the ground)

I was like…what is going on? What's wrong with him?

Me: *What?*

Boss: (still laughing): *So she needs light bulbs!* (and he stressed the word light).

Me: *Yes, that's what I said.*

Boss: *No, you said boobs.* (and pointed to his body repeating the word again and finished). *You scared me. If she needed boobs we can't do anything but now that I know it is light bulbs you can go ahead and change the bulbs for her…* (and he laughed again because he said bulbs like I did.)

Me: *I didn't say that.*

Boss: *Yes you did.*

Me: *No, I didn't.*

Boss: *Yes, you did. Say bulb.*

Me: *I won't say it.*

Boss: *Come on, say it.*

Me: *Bulb.*

Boss: *No... You are saying boob. Repeat with me: BUUULB.*

So, that's how I found out the difference between bulbs and boobs.

We kept going up the street and he was still looking at me and smiling he said, "You are so cute."
We laughed and he hugged me and we went back to the office.

And NO, that was not sexual harassment.

∞

Watching baseball with my husband:

Me: *Hey Honey, tell me about this thing...how does it work?*

He tells me in his way that I can't comprehend and I say:

"So, there are many positions: Pitcher, Catcher, First Base, Second Base, Third Base, Short Stop, Center Field, Left Field, Right Field... and there is Home Run."

Husband, not really paying attention to me: *Right.*

Me: *Why do they name dog out, the place for the players?*

Husband: *It's underground. They dig the ground.*

Me: *What does dog has to do with it?*

Husband: *It's dugout... from digging.*

Me: *Oh, dig, dug... dugout! I see.*

As you can see, it's the language barrier I always talk about.

∞

One day, my husband and I were coming back from Arizona and there is a border patrol point check near El Centro, actually, it's closer to San Diego than El Centro and we had to stop for the immigration.

134

It was around 6 or 7 pm and it was dark and I saw a bunch of "birds" flying around and I said to my husband, *"Look, there is a bunch of those vampire birds!"*

And he simply replied, *"Bats?"*

And I was all excited and said, *"Yes, bats!"*

I always say things like this and the good thing is that my husband understands me. Well… most of the time.

∞

Yesterday we went out for walk and drive in Encinitas and we stopped at his new favorite place he just discovered a couple of weeks ago in Sacramento to buy us a shake and we were coming back home and I said: *Ouch, I have a frozen brain!*

And he said: *You have a brain freeze.*

See, I'm still messing up my words here and there and that's why I was not offered a job.

∞

I love rejection. Seriously!!

Being an actor you will most likely be rejected in 90% of the jobs you will submit for.

I think I got thick-skinned because of all the rejection I got searching for jobs when I first arrived.

Now, being rejected as an actor doesn't bother me as much and we actors know that audition does not guarantee we will get the job. Many actors get depressed because of that. It's very hard to accept that but for me it's as natural as having an accent, being from another country or even region.

∞

135

Here is the end of my adventure writing this book. I don't make long-term plans. I try to live one day at a time. I don't know when I'm getting off this train called life.
As I said before, I don't know what the future holds for me. All I know is that I'm pretty happy with my actual situation and, as for the future, I trust the Universe. I guess I should say I trust God.

One thing I can say, though. I miss my mother so much. I really wish she were here and I choose to believe that she is always with me in spirit. She is for sure in my heart. I'm a part of her. She still lives in me and in my siblings and I will carry her love and teaching with me for the rest of my life.

Thank you so much for reading this book. I really hope you enjoyed reading it and learning a little about me and my little saga.

Part of all the proceeds of this book will go to non-profit organizations and to causes that I believe in.

Blessings to all of you!

Obrigada!
Isabel Canzoneri

Isabel Canzoneri

www.isabelcanzoneri.com
@icanzoneri

Made in the USA
San Bernardino, CA
23 December 2016